Ya...
But How?

Ya...
But How?

ONLINE PLATFORM BUILDING
FOR THE VERY, VERY BEGINNER!

Melanie Fischer

ISBN: 1511632569
ISBN 13: 9781511632560
Library of Congress Control Number: 2015905606
CreateSpace Independent Publishing Platform
North Charleston, South Carolina

What people are saying about *Ya…But How?*

"Melanie, your approach to writing is unique and utterly engaging. I can't wait until your techie book is released—not just for the tech stuff, but for the fun of reading it!"

Bobbi Junior – Author of "The Reluctant Caregiver"
bobbijunior.com

"I love your writing voice. And, as your guinea pig, I can testify to the fact that your book *Ya … But How?* will be what many many people need and will gobble up!"

Joylene M Bailey – Blogs at ScrapsOfJoy.com

"I am the type of person who loves instructions in easy, basic, form. When reading through *Ya…But How?* the chapters were simple and I received all the instruction I needed easily and effectively. Thanks Melanie. Now I do know how!!"

Shelley Jogola –An un-tetchy friend

This book is dedicated to all of those who recognize they need to get their purposeful works into the world, and are determined to do so.

Table of Contents

Before the Beginning xv

Chapter 1   A Little Background Before We Get Started 1

Section ONE: Putting On Your Tool Belt 5

Chapter 2   Solidifying the Plan 6
                  a) Gaining Vision and Clarity 6
                  b) Write it Down 7

Chapter 3   Standing Your Ground with Technology. 9
                  a) Technology…Not for the Faint of Heart!. 9
                  b) Using Your Resources. 10

Chapter 4   A Little Pep-Talk Before We Begin 12

Section TWO: Laying the Planks 15

Chapter 5   Plank 1: Website. 17
                  a) Website Options 18
                  b) Building Your Website 29
                  c) Developing Your Website. 41
                  d) Designing Your Website. 45

Chapter 6   Plank 2: Blog 50
              a) Blogging with *Blogger* 51
              b) Blogging with *WordPress.com* 53
              c) Blogging with *WordPress.org* 54

Chapter 7   Plank 3: Opt-In Boxes 57
              a) What is an Opt-In Box? 57
              b) What is an Email Marketing Service? 58
              c) Sign Up With an Email Marketing Service 58
              d) Setting Up a List 59
              e) Create and Install an Opt-In Box
                 On a Static Page 61
              f) Enable People to Sign Up For Your Blog 63
              g) Install an Opt-In Box for Your Blog onto
                 Your Blog Page 65
              h) Creating Broadcasts 67
              i) Creating a Follow Up Series 69

Chapter 8   Plank 4: Social Media 73
              a) Some Social Media Channels 74
              b) How to Create a Facebook Author or
                 Business Page 75
              c) How to Get Set Up on Twitter 77
              d) Get Set Up with LinkedIn 78
              e) Setting Up on Pinterest 79
              f) Activating the Social Media Buttons on
                 Your Website 80
              g) Installing Social Media Buttons 82
              h) Some Notes on Social Media 83
              i) Social Networking for Writers and Readers 83

Chapter 9   Plank 5: Video 85
              a) Setting Up on YouTube 86
              b) Making Videos and Uploading
                 Them to YouTube 87
              c) A Little More YouTube Video Info 88

            d) Creating a Book Trailer 89

            e) Putting Your Videos onto Your Website 90

Section THREE: Wrapping It Up 95

Chapter 10   Wrap It Up 96

            a) Would You Give a Book Review? 97

            b) Ya...But Now What? 99

Resources 103

Other Resources 105

Glossary 107

Acknowledgments 111

Notes 114

Before the Beginning

You are peering into a book that is offering to help you build a bridge from having little or no online presence, to existing online in a meaningful way. An online presence is often referred to as an **online platform**. This term *online platform* is used as an umbrella term to describe the combination of all the online devices which are being used to help make your works known. A **platform** typically has two parts 1) The *physical components,* such as: a blog, podcast and social media channels 2) The *people* whom you have influence on, such as: members of a group or a club you are part of, your social media followers, blog subscribers and podcast listeners. Your platform ultimately is the *people* you have influence on, but without the physical means of reaching out, it would be difficult to connect with them.

Considering that you have this material in your hands, I suspect you are in the shoes of having little knowledge about how to build your online platform. I was in similar shoes not long ago—they can feel a bit clunky and may seem too big to fill. Building an online platform may appear to be a task only for the "techy" folks. However, if the required steps are laid out in a manageable fashion, these are shoes that even the least tech savvy person can grow into.

Why is it important for some of us to figure out how to build an online platform? Because for a portion of us, this is what will assist in pursuing our purpose. Not everyone's purpose includes being online. But if this *is* part of the plan for your life, it is very helpful to be walked through the process rather than having to muddle through it on your own.

I have a solid belief that we are all created for a purpose, and writing is a big part of mine. I felt that I needed a way to share the messages that are in my writings, so an online platform was an inevitable part of my life journey. With a fear of anything electronic, and one of the last people in my family to even get a cell phone, I was the least likely candidate to venture into the online world. But I was eager to achieve what I trusted was part of my life plan, so I needed to do what it took to get there. I had to figure the "techy" stuff out. I plowed through the forest of information and miraculously managed to put together a website, along with other platform pieces. By the time I knocked down the final tree, I had a stack of notes that I did not have the heart to throw away.

Each person is clothed with gifts, skills, abilities and aspirations, yet much of these are not being shared because so many people are stuck in a place of not knowing how to get where they gotta go. They end up throwing their arms up in the air, crying out "Ya...But How?" It is not that there is a lack of material out there, but for those who have no idea where to start, the abundance of information becomes overwhelming.

I am passionate about equipping people to live their purpose. Purpose is *not* fulfilled by standing helplessly in the gulley of "Ya... But How?" This is why I compiled my stack of notes and created this workbook for you.

CHAPTER 1

A Little Background Before We Get Started

M any of us know where we are (point A: *a.k.a* lost) and we may have an idea, or at least somewhat of an idea, of where we aim to go (point B: *a.k.a* found). However, we end up falling in the giant gap in between. I call this gap, "Ya...But How?" Sadly, there are a lot of great works that are not being shared, and many people who are not living their purpose, purely because the author or creator of those efforts does not know *how* to send his works into the world. When a bridge is built across this gully, needs can be met and great purpose can be found.

You will learn how to build a bridge across the canyon of "Ya... But How?" one plank at a time as you are walked through the steps (excluding the back-steps and side-steps), that I took to build my online platform. Being a writer, my teachings will lean towards writers, but this information can be used for any sector. An online presence is an important piece in gaining visibility no matter what your works are.

In order to have a presence you need to have some sort of stage to perform on. This is often referred to as a platform; more specifically an online platform if you are presenting your works to the World Wide Web. A combination of methods for getting your works known will make up your stage. For instance, a website is a great place to start for organizing and sharing your ideas, products and services. A blog may be added to your website in order to continuously generate new ideas and share information. Also, it is a good idea to include social media (*Facebook, Twitter* etc.) in your platform as it is a way to expand your reach.

We have just talked about some of the physical components of a platform, but ultimately a platform is made up of people. After all, it is *people* who are behind the social networks, the websites and the blogs. There may be individuals who are already a part of your platform—people whom you have influence on. Examples of such audiences are hobby groups, your businesses clients, church or other community groups.

For the purpose of this book though, we are going to focus on setting up certain *physical components* of your online platform. Once you move through this material and the pieces are in place, then you will be ready to move onto increasing your audience. You may choose to later expand your platform to include book publishing, podcasts, webinars, public speaking and more. For now we will stick to some simple, and potentially important pieces of an online platform and then you can build onto it as you see fit. You are not confined to the walls of "everyone is doing it that way so I must do it that way." Get started, then use your knowledge, passions, skills and life experiences to grow your platform. Step outside of the box and you will reach people you would have never thought possible.

Knowing that you need a platform in order to expand your reach is one thing, actually building it is another. If you have attempted to sift through the information available on how to build an online platform, you have likely discovered that it feels similar to opening an airplane door in midflight; you get sucked out, never to return. Not to fret! Rather than having to navigate your way through a jungle without a map, I am going to walk you through what it takes to build your online platform. Chances are you would rather spend more time performing your craft than building the stage to perform it on.

Let's not spend any more time staring under the hood. Lather on the elbow grease and let's get started.

Note: This book is a layout of the steps which I learned and implemented in order to build my online platform. There are many ways to build an online platform. This book teaches several of the steps which can be taken, but may not necessarily provide the best choices for *your* specific needs. Discernment is a necessity in determining your direction and in choosing the products and services that will best suit your needs.

SECTION ONE:

Putting On Your Tool Belt

You will need to put on your tool belt before we start collecting the tools required to build the bridge across the gully of "Ya… But How?"

Although our focus is going to be on the "hows," gaining some clarity on "why" you plan to do this will increase your odds of sticking to it. This section will focus on the "whys," which will add hardener to the "hows" and solidify your plan.

Speaking of tools in your tool belt, there is a *glossary* at the end of this book if you get hung up on the terminology along the way.

CHAPTER 2

Solidifying the Plan

a) Gaining Vision and Clarity

I strongly believe in doing what we are created to do, so I personally spent an immense amount of time in thought and prayer over the focus of my life. I encourage you to do the same. When one is fuelled by true passion and God given direction, the chances of making it to the finish line before we run out of gas is much greater. Being fuelled by wishes and good ideas without a backbone of true purpose would be like trying to run a gas engine on diesel fuel: the vehicle would start, but would run poorly.

Gaining vision and clarity will help keep you on track, and will save you from unnecessary frustrations. *Vision* is the perceived picture of what the project will look like when it all comes together. It will help you understand who your target audience is, it will keep you focused, and will direct your venture when developing logos, colours, style, blog topics and so on. *Clarity* is simplifying things, and understanding the pieces of the bigger picture.

Vision and clarity helped immensely in developing my business brand. For instance, my business endeavour is called *Hungry for Purpose,* therefore I follow a theme of food analogies throughout. I drop *crumbs of purpose* (mini inspirations) in the email inboxes of subscribers every few days. Also, my logo is a bowl of "purpose," appropriate to the business venture title (you will find my logo on the back of this book).

Maintaining a blog, website, email lists, and whatever other tools you choose to use will take dedication. Be sure to do some exploring to ensure that having an online presence is in fact part of your life picture.

Once you have a general vision and basic clarity, assuming that an online presence is part of it, you are ready to move ahead.

b) Write it Down

Personally, I design everything on paper first. Perhaps this is because I am drawn to the art of writing, or maybe it is because I need to switch my tactics in order to entertain my attention span of a kindergartner on a sugar fix. A pen and paper has a way of connecting us to what we are writing down, and gives us a means to draw out a plan in a manner which is not as easy to do on a computer. However, a word document, spreadsheet or many other mediums would certainly work. Just choose whatever suits you best.

Begin by drawing out, the best you can, your vision for your online platform. Do you see a blog as part of the plan? What about videos? Will you be selling books or any other products or services? What is the message that you desire to share? The clearer you are in your vision, the straighter the path to your destination, but be cautious not to obsess over every detail before you begin. A general direction is necessary; requiring exact coordinates will paralyze you.

Your vision, focus and purpose will develop further as you press onward. Your direction will become clearer as you pay attention to the process and are intentional in your steps forward. Things will come together if you are eager, but patient, to learn and grow along the way.

I suggest that you make the corner of your desk a home to a stack of loose-leaf paper with ever-evolving diagrams, goals and clarifications of your online platform and, more generally, your life purpose and direction. Or create an ever-evolving file on your computer or tablet if you prefer. It would not make sense to try and build a house without blueprints, so why try to build your vocation without some sort of plan?

If you have little understanding of the vision for your online platform, it would be a good idea to read through this book entirely before beginning the actual setup steps. Having an understanding of how the pieces fit together, before you start building, may smoothen out any wrinkles of confusion.

CHAPTER 3

Standing Your Ground with Technology

a) Technology...Not for the Faint of Heart!

A plan that involves embracing technology to any degree requires eating perseverance for breakfast.

When dealing with technology you need to be more stubborn than the issue at hand. Tackling the "techy" beast is not for the faint of heart, but the rewards are great if you persist. Technology is a tricky opponent; keep at it, use your resources, keep the end in mind, and you will have victory!

If something just WILL NOT WORK, take a break! Sometimes we get a bit eager and end up typing in an incorrect password. Many sites will temporarily lock you out if the wrong password is entered several times, which can easily happen if you pelt the ENTER key with your index finger ten times in a row out of frustration. Trust me, I have almost worn out that button. If you step away from what you are doing for fifteen minutes or so, often things will reset. Or, perhaps it is our brains that need to reset. Either way, this "techy" stuff tends to make more sense after taking a breather.

Warning:

The use of this mighty thing called technology can cause delusions—delusions that it is fantastic and will always work. Then reality kicks in and introduces the fact that technology will never *always* work. Things working "well" may be unexpectedly attacked by sneaky cyber bugs or other irritants. However, smashing the computer will not fix it.

b) Using Your Resources

It would be impossible for me, or anyone, to foresee and address every hurdle that will come your way, because the path will be different for each person. The most practical approach for you to navigate your way through online platform building (or anything for that fact), is to deal with one specific issue at a time. You likely do not eat an entire meal in a single bite, so don't attempt to undertake all issues that you face in a single bite either or you may choke. Once one particular challenge is resolved, then you can move to the next challenge.

There is a lot to learn about all this online "techy" stuff, and there is a ton of information out there; it would not make sense to re-create all of the material that already exists. There will be times when I will send you out to do further research online. I will point you in the direction and try my best to remove the blindfold so you can see where you are going.

If you get stuck on something or require more information and greater details, don't *give* up, *look it* up! There may be videos and resources provided with particular services. Most of your paid services will have a help desk, so call it if you need to. You can also use a search engine like *Google* to look for solutions. *Google* can be very useful, even some web designers who are trained in code and the whole shebang use it.

You can develop your relationship with *Google* by searching for experts in a particular field, blogs on a specific topic, or forums and discussion panels where you can ask questions and dig for answers.

For example, type the topic or question that you are stuck on into the *Google* search box…such as "blogs on blogging" or "expert advice on choosing a blog topic" or "why should I blog?" You may have to go through the search results a bit in order to find the answer that you are looking for, but keep digging and you will almost always find the answers to your question.

There is always an option to pay for services or tasks if you get stuck on something or if you just don't have the time or patience to figure out a particular step. You can either use the paid support that is offered by specific service providers, or you can choose to use other web support services.

There are heaps of services to choose from. In order to narrow down your search a bit, you can check out the list of resources at the end of this book, or head over to my website resource page:

http://www.hungryforpurpose.com/resources

CHAPTER 4

A Little Pep-Talk
Before We Begin

B efore pounding in the first nail of your online platform, let's have a little chat. There is a ton of information and various interpretations of what a platform is. We could dive deep into this topic but then we would risk the possibility of being afflicted by The Bends (an excruciatingly painful disorder that divers get when going too deep and coming up too quickly). This is a book for beginners so we are going to stay in the shallow end and keep things as simple as possible.

We touched on what a platform is in chapter one, but we are going to review it a bit here before we get started building it. In the most straightforward terms, *a platform is a stage to perform on*. Of course you are going to want an audience eventually, but our focus throughout our time together will be to build the actual stage. Just like a celebrity often switches things up from a physical stage to perform on, to a TV program or a movie screen in order to expand their reach, it is a good idea to be seen in a few different places. You have many online platform options, such as social media, a website, a blog and more. It is important to use various means to gain an audience, but do not try too many things at once or you will get stretched so thin you may snap.

There may very well be as many ways to create an online presence as there are people online. I encourage you to explore, modify and get creative with the following steps in building an online platform. Your products, your style, simply *you*, are different than everyone else, so your platform should be different too! This workbook is not intended to make a "cookie-cutter-me." It is meant to equip you with tools in order to help you move toward your calling so *you* can be *you* in order to fulfill your own unique purpose!

The guidance in this book is here to get you started on your online "techy" journey, but it certainly is not intended to be the end. Pursuing your own venture will take persistence to get it started and discipline to keep it going. We all know that life drops obstacles on our paths along the way, so expect them. The roadblocks are often NOT the biggest problem...it is "not pursuing a detour" that truly stops us from moving forward. Continuously *seeking* your direction, being *intentional* in your movement forward, and *persevering* will be the most valuable tools in your tool belt.

SECTION TWO:

Laying the Planks

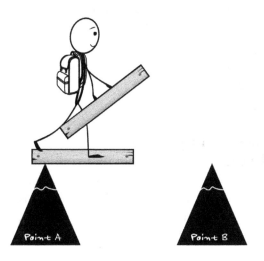

So here you are, standing at "Point A." In order to get to "Point B" you will need to lay the planks across the canyon of "Ya... But How?" Each "plank" will be a significant piece of your online platform. Keep at it and you will be on the other side in no time.

Keep in mind as you work through this book that technology is constantly changing. Applications, services and providers are always updating. It is impossible to *keep up* with all of the changes, so rather, *work with it*. The video tutorials and step-by-step instructions are based on the steps at the time this book was put together. By the time you get to it there may have been some changes. For the most part, the changes will be minor and you will have no problem working around it. But if you come across a step that just doesn't make sense, you can look for instructions on the website of the service that you are working on, search the web for instructions, or depending on which service you are working with there may be a help desk that you can contact for assistance. Always remember to persevere—the more experience you get with this "techy" stuff, the more comfortable you will become, and the easier it will be to work with.

To access the videos within this book, either: 1) click on the active website link if you are viewing this in a format that allows you to do so (such as an e-reader) 2) type the provided links into a web browser, or 3) scan the QR codes. A QR (Quick Response) code is a scanable image that is most often an array of odd looking black and white squares that make up a larger square. QR codes can be scanned with a smart phone or tablet that is equipped with a camera. First you will need to download a QR-code app. You will find such an app for free in the app store for whichever smartphone or tablet you are using.

As you work your way through the following instructions, there are going to be choices that you will need to make along the way. Your choices will depend on the direction that you intend your platform to go. You may make the best choice, or you may not—that is a part of learning. Do your best to understand your options, and then do the work that is necessary for the choices you make. A misstep may add unnecessary time to your journey, but a step never taken will get you nowhere at all.

Let's begin!

CHAPTER 5

Plank 1: Website

We are going to start with a website as the first "plank" to your online platform. A website is like a piece of online property. Think of needing a website like a farmer needs a piece of land. The farmer needs land in order to plant seeds in his field. You need a piece of *virtual land* in order to plant information onto the World Wide Web. A website is a good place to start because you can use it as the center of your platform and link all of your other web activity to it.

A website allows you to categorize your information by *pages*. In a similar way, a farmer has different pieces of land for various purposes: the farmer may have a field of oats, a field of wheat and a field of corn. It is the same farmer and the same farm, but there are different strips of land for different purposes. Likewise, a website can have a home page, a sales page and a page for a blog—same author, same website but different pages for different types of content.

There are generally two types of website pages: A **Static Page** and a **Blog Page**. The content on a static page generally stays the same. Content on a blog page is typically continually added. New entries to a blog are referred to as *posts*. Examples of static pages would be a *contact* page and an *about* page. If there are changes to a *static page* it would generally replace the existing information (such as a change of address); whereas the *blog page* is like an online journal where new content (entries) are added and the old content remains available. The old posts are usually archived by date, topics and keywords.

A website is also a place where followers can sign up to receive regular information from you. Another handy use for a website is to link your social media sites to it so people can find you in *all* the places online that you are present.

As you can see, a website gives you many avenues to build and plenty of opportunities to let your creativity out of its pen. Your imagination does not need to have lines as straight as the edges of a farmer's field.

a) Website Options

A farmer will need to have living quarters on his property. He will have different options of how to build his home, just like you will have different options when building your website. You could build a website right from scratch by using code, which would be similar to a master carpenter being able to design and build a house from scratch; that would take a vast amount of knowledge and experience. Since this farmer is less experienced than a master builder, we are going to use a website building tool that has the structure in place for us. The website building tool that is generally used in order to allow the less techy folks to create websites is called a *CMS*. A **CMS (Content Management System)** is a web application that makes it easy to add, edit and manage your website. This would be a bit like using a prefabricated home for the structure of your house—the basics are put together for you. You will then just need to tailor it to your liking and add the finishing touches. Just like you would have choices for different prefabricated home builders, you also have choices for different website builders.

We are going to visit just three of the most popular website builders so this doesn't become overwhelming. It will depend on the vision of your endeavour as to which choice will be best for you.

The three website building possibilities that we will be looking at are 1) Blogger (also known as *BlogSpot)* 2) WordPress.com 3) WordPress.org The first two we will only visit briefly. We will then spend the majority of our time talking about *WordPress.org* because it is the website option that provides the most diversity and generally requires the most amount of guidance. I highly recommend that you read the following information on all three of these website building options, as well as do some additional research on the pros and cons of each, before making a decision on which one to go with.

Before we move forward with learning more about these three website building choices, you need to know a term: *Web hosting*. **Web hosting** means having your website stored (hosted) on a *server* in order for it to be accessed over the internet. A **server** is basically a tower of computer-like hardware that exists somewhere—wherever that may be. You don't need to concern yourself with this in detail. All you need to know is that every website needs to sit on a server in order for it to be accessed over the internet.

Websites generally fit into one of two categories: **Hosted website** or **Self-hosted website**. A hosted website is a website that hosting on a server is provided for you. A Self-hosted website is a website that you have to find hosting for yourself, and therefore a self-hosted website does NOT provide hosting on a server for you.

To help explain the difference between these two, imagine this... let's say you own a house trailer. You have a problem though. The trailer is sitting on skids in the middle of the street because you do not have anywhere to put it. You have two choices. First, your good friend Doris tells you that her Uncle Bob has a piece of property that you can put your trailer on for free. This may seem like a good idea, but when you get there, there is a giant advertising billboard on your front lawn for Uncle Bob's business, and the soil out back is not suitable for you to plant your dream garden. You are not paying for this land though, so you can't be too choosy. Also, if Uncle Bob decides to change his mind, your trailer is back out on the street (assuming that you get your trailer back at all). Your second choice is to rent a piece of property, pay the fees, and maintain it yourself.

A hosted website is like the first choice. There are many factors which you do not control, and the possibility of losing your content if there are discrepancies is higher. This option is free though (unless you want to upgrade), and the maintenance of the land is taken care of for you.

A Self-hosted website is like the second choice. You have control over many more factors in such a situation, but for a fee. The maintenance on the land is all up to you though. For the most part, as long as you pay your rent, your trailer has a home. Of course there are still some rules, but there is much more flexibility as to what you can do with your website land.

There are certainly pros and cons to both scenarios. We will go into some details of the pros and cons that relate specifically to different website options.

Ok. Let's get into the three website building options that we are going to cover. Keep in mind that each one will fit into one of the two categories: 1. Hosted website 2. Self-hosted website.

1) Blogger

Blogger is primarily intended for blogging, but may be used as a website also. The default when first setting up a *Blogger* site is a single blogging page. Static pages may be added in order to use *Blogger* as a traditional website. *Blogger* is a hosted website, and is owned by *Google*. Being that it is a hosted site, it is free—the basics are free, but you can pay for upgrades.

When you set up with blogger, your website name will automatically tack on "blogspot." The website name is often referred to as the **domain name**. The terms *website name*, *domain name* and *web address* tend to be used interchangeably. When using Blogger, you can upgrade and choose your own domain name. This would allow you to have "blogspot" removed from your website name. This would give your blog a more professional feel. For example: *www.yourname.blogspot.com* would change to *www.yourname.com*

We will touch on choosing a domain name a little later on.

Pros of using *Blogger* for your website:

It is free (there are paid upgrades available, but the basics are free).
It is quick to set up and get started.
It is easy to set up and run, and requires little technical knowhow.
Links to your social media sites can easily be activated on *Blogger*.
Much of the security updates, spam protection and back-end maintenance are done for you.

Cons of using *Blogger* for your website:

You do not own this website, *Google* does (*Blogger* is owned by *Google*). *Google* operates *Blogger* and can block your access to it or shut it down at any time.

Blogger has very specific tools which you can access to use for your site, but you cannot expand them to meet other needs; your marketing potential with such a site is therefore limited.

Blogger only has a limited selection of templates available for you to use. You can make basic adjustments to your layout (such as colour and some font changes), but are unable to make any major modifications.

There are limitations when it comes to image storage.

The blog's web address will have the name "blogspot" in it which gives the website an unprofessional feel (unless you pay for an upgrade to purchase your domain name, and therefore have "blogspot" removed).

Overall professionalism may lack when using this website building option. This is not a big deal if you are using your website for a personal blog, but you may face some challenges if you are using it for an extensive business venture.

The ability to move your *Blogger* site to a different type of website (such as *WordPress*) is a complicated job, and there is a significant risk that you will lose subscribers and ranking when doing so.

There is limited support for *Blogger,* besides the basic documentation and a user's forum.

WordPress websites

Now we are going to get into the website building tool *WordPress*. There is a bit more to explain here than there was with *Blogger*, so we are going to have to go down a few rabbit trails. It might seem like we are jumping all over the place, but it will come together…just stay with me.

First, let me fill you in a bit on *WordPress* in general before we talk specifically about *WordPress.com* and *WordPress.org*. *WordPress* is a commonly used CMS. Due to its popularity, there is a ton of information online that you can turn to if you get stuck, which makes this a good choice for website building.

WordPress in itself is what is called *open source software*, which is software that the source code can be modified by programmers. This often means that anyone can use this software and it is free. In the case of *WordPress* it is free; both free to use and free of charge (the basic software is free—there are paid options, upgrades and additions available).

Now this is where it gets a bit confusing. There is a fork here in the online platform building road because there are two forms of *WordPress* (both owned by the same company): *WordPress.com* and *WordPress.org*

No need to shackle you to confusion, so let's clear something up right here. The two forms of *WordPress* (.org & .com) **DOES NOT** determine whether your website has .com or .org at the end.

The basic difference between *WordPress.com* and *WordPress.org* is that *WordPress.com* provides hosting on a server for you (a hosted site) and *WordPress.org* does not (a self-hosted site).

Being that *WordPress.com* is a hosted site, this cyber property is *lent* to you and is therefore free and will require little work to setup and begin. *WordPress.org* on the other hand will require you to "rent" land to put *WordPress* onto. When you rent property you have a landlord. Your cyber landlord is called a **web host provider.** You will need to obtain your own web host provider and will need to pay for them to host your website for you. Don't worry I will show you how to do this.

A little side note: The word "self-hosted" in the above context means that you have to find your own web host provider, but this word is not technically the correct word because self-hosted would truly mean "self" hosted. To actually host a site yourself you would need your own server (expensive computer stuff) and more knowhow than *I* know how. The word "paid-hosted" would be the correct word to use because you are paying a web host provider to host your website.

However, "self-hosted" is the word most commonly used to describe "paid-hosting," so I will use the wording self-hosting/self-hosted so as to minimize confusion.

Quick recap: There are generally two categories of websites, hosted and self-hosted. Hosted sites are free for the basic service. *Blogger* and *WordPress.com* are hosted sites. Self-hosted means that you are responsible for having your website hosted for you, and there is a cost for this service. *WordPress.org* is a self-hosted site.

You may be asking "why would I use a self-hosted site when I have to pay for the service and it sounds more confusing to set up?" There are many advantages to having a self-hosted site. *WordPress.org* is like *owning* the home that is on the land, as opposed to *renting* the home. Owning the home gives you significantly more freedom with the potential of it, but the upkeep is all up to you (unless you hire someone to keep it up for you). *WordPress.com* is more like rental property so there are less maintenance headaches but much less freedom as to what you can do with the property. You can't just punch out walls and renovate; you will have to work with basic templates and will only be able to make simple alterations.

There is quite the debate as to which is better, *WordPress.com* or *WordPress*.org. I will give an overview of both, and let you decide which website (if either) would work best for you. Your choice will largely depend on the direction of your endeavour. Let's take a look at both in greater detail.

2) *WordPress.com*

WordPress.com is the second of the three options that we are going to look at for website building. I have already explained that *WordPress.com* is a hosted site, and you now know what that means.

We will dig into the pros and cons of *WordPress.com* and *WordPress.org* so that when you choose which website building peg to drive into the ground you will have more understanding to latch onto.

Pros of using *WordPress.com* for your website:

The basic service is free (there are upgrades available for a cost).
This website is already on a server, therefore web hosting is provided for you.
Automatic spam-protection, automatic back-up and security and back-end maintenance is provided.
Very little technical knowhow is required to begin using this website—you basically sign-up, set-up and start-up.

Cons of using *WordPress.com* for your website:

The professionalism of a *WordPress.com* site is questionable because the web address will have the actual words "*WordPress*" in it (unless you pay for an upgrade).
Third party ads will pop up unless you pay for the option of disallowing this. Links that advertise *WordPress.com* and their products cannot be removed.
There are restrictions on selling advertising space for the website.
You do not own this website, so you run the risk of it being shutdown at any time.
Some video and advanced picture capabilities may be more limiting on such a website.
At the time of this publication, it is not possible to place an *opt-in box* directly onto a *WordPress.com* site; therefore, email marketing which is used for building lists is limited. (You will learn about opt-in boxes and email marketing in chapter 7).
Except for a few paid options, *plugins* cannot be installed on a *WordPress.com* site; therefore there are many limitations to such a site. A **plugin** is an additional piece of software that can be installed on a website in order to add features and modifications. Examples of plugins are shopping carts, photo galleries and specific video formats.

Note: *WordPress.com* has been working on expanding their capabilities, so you may find they are increasingly offering tools that are furthering the potential of a *WordPress.com* website.

3) *WordPress.org*

So here we are at the third option for website building. Some of this can be a bit confusing so it doesn't hurt to review it again. *WordPress.org* is a self-hosted site, therefore you will need to pay a web host provider a monthly fee to host your website for you. *WordPress. org* does require more work than the other two options but you will have much greater freedom in the design of your website and will have greater marketing potential. A *WordPress.org* website has the most options for optimizing your online presence. And once again, a *WordPress.org* site does NOT mean that ".org" will be at the end of your website name.

Pros of using *WordPress.org* for your website:

WordPress.org means that you own the website that you have purchased the domain name for; you would therefore never have the name "wordpress" in your website name.

Since, with *WordPress* you would own your own website, you do not run as high of a risk of the service being discontinued or your website being shut down.

Advertisements will only pop-up if you *choose* to advertise on your site.

You will have the ability to install limitless plugins.

Opt-in boxes (which will be explained in chapter 7) for email campaigning can be installed in order for people to sign up to receive your content.

WordPress.org gives you much more wiggle room for marketing and list building.

There is little limit to what you can do with this website, assuming that you have the skill or are willing to seek the knowledge or assistance.

Note: There are still policies that you need to agree with and follow when using a self-hosted site such as *WordPress.org*, but there is much more freedom with a self-hosted site than with a hosted site.

Cons of using *WordPress.org* for your website:

WordPress.org is a "do-it-yourself" type of website which can be a pro or con, depending on if you are willing and able to put in the extra work.

You will need to pay for a web host provider (usually around $7 - $15/ month) and also pay for your domain name (typically a yearly fee).

You will need to maintain your own security and backups. The web host provider will typically have information available on how to do this.

You are responsible for all of your own web maintenance. Like owning your own house, if the furnace breaks down you will need to fix it or pay someone to fix it. For instance, if a page on your website is not displaying, you would need to go into the **back-end** of your website and do some troubleshooting in order to resolve the issue yourself. (The back-end is where you will be making all of your changes—this is an area which is not accessible to the general public.)

You are responsible for upgrades (you will most likely be notified when these need to be done, and for the most part this can be done in one or two clicks).

Recap on the discussed website options:

WordPress.com and *Blogger* are hosted websites: a hosted website is hosted for you, which means these are free website building options (the basics are free, there are paid upgrades available). You do not own a hosted website though, therefore there is a risk that the site could be shut down at any time. Hosted sites are generally quick and easy to set up and get started. They require little technical knowledge to maintain but have greater limitations.

WordPress.org is a website that you would own so you would not run the same degree of risk in having your website shut down. You will however need to pay to have your website hosted on a server. A *WordPress.org* site requires more upkeep; you will be responsible for upgrades, security and other website maintenance. With a *WordPress. org* website you would have much more freedom and possibilities when it comes to business transactions, marketing, advertising, and email campaigns.

Decisions, decisions!

I know, I know! There is a lot of information to sift through and many important choices to make. I recall feeling as if my head was being put in a vice at this point in the game. Push on and it will come together.

There are many people who have gone before you, so there is much advice online from the pioneers. Do some reading, talk to people you know who already have a website, and weigh the pros & cons. Most importantly, pay attention to what your purpose is and what the vision is for your online platform, and then go for the option that suits *you* best.

I caution you about making the decision purely based on cost. When a farmer purchases a piece of property, he does so as a business investment. He uses the land that he buys to yield a crop from the seeds he sows in order to be profitable. If you are seeking to position yourself as a published author or an established artist or business owner, you will have more options for creative growth with a self-hosted website. Remember though, a self-hosted site takes more of a commitment to maintain. Serious bloggers and online entrepreneurs tend to take the *WordPress.org* route.

There are instances though when *WordPress.com* or *Blogger* would be a better fit. Examples of such cases would be: if your emphasis is on blogging without a heavy focus on marketing, or if you plan to use your website as a place to display content for an audience such as your family or friends. There are as well, some authors who use the *WordPress.com* or *Blogger* option. *WordPress.com* and *Blogger* are fairly easy to set up and maintain, so if you find that one of these is a good option for you there is no need to make more work for yourself than necessary.

If you find yourself becoming paralyzed by the choices and the learning curve, a *WordPress.com* site is an excellent place to dabble, practice, learn the ropes, and figure out your focus. The back-end of both types of *WordPress* are similar, so this would give you an opportunity to gain some hands-on learning with *WordPress*. You could then later set up a *WordPress.org* website if you see it necessary.

Note: It *is* possible to transfer a hosted website to a self-hosted website, although it is a bit of a hassle and you run the risk of losing followers, ranking and content. If you choose to go with a hosted site with the sense of later transferring to a *WordPress.org* site, it will be easier to transfer a *WordPress.com* site than a *Blogger* site because the two forms of *WordPress* are more compatible with one another.

b) Building Your Website

Choosing your website name

Before you can actually start building your website you need to have a name for it because people need to know where to find you online. Just like your home has an address, so does your website. Your followers will find your website by typing your web address into a web browser. The web address will look something like this: www.websitename.com

When you get to the step of setting up your website, you will need to be ready with a web address of your choice. Remember that a web address is commonly called a domain name.

Note: The terms *website, web address, domain* and *URL* all tend to be used interchangeably. **URL** stands for (uniform resource locator). Your URL is your web address, which is also your domain name.

Every website has a different address, therefore the domain (website name) that you choose will need to be original. This in itself can be a little tricky as there are millions of websites. Even if you think you have come up with a unique name, you may be surprised that someone else has already come up with it. Many people simply use their own name, but even that can be challenging, as there could be others in the world with your same name. One solution is to tack on a title such as "writer," "coach," "blogger," "artist," after your name.

An example of this would be www.yourname**artist**.com

One quick way to check if your idea for a website name is taken is to do a quick online search. Just plug your desired name into a search engine like *Google* and see if a website with that name comes up.

Some web host providers, such as *GoDaddy*, have a domain search tool right on their website so you can plug in a desired domain name right there to see if it is available before you get your heart set on it.

Some people will say that your domain is incredibly important and others will say not to get hung up on the details as it is more important to choose a name and get started than to have no website and never start.

I personally put a lot of thought and prayer into choosing my domain name. The name of your website is going to be a name that you will want your potential followers/clients/customers to identify with and remember. It would be much more inconvenient to start over with a new domain name later than it is to do some exploring first.

When choosing your name it is a good idea to stay away from funky spelling and cutesy mixes of numbers and letters—such as 4get (forget) or l8er (later)—unless funky spelling would truly benefit you in your endeavour. If your web address is confusing at all you may have to explain it every time you give it out. Also, your website likely will not come to the top when an interested customer or follower tries to find you by searching the web by your website name if the 'incorrect' spelling is used. Remember that you want people to find you, so try your best not to be a needle in a haystack.

Choosing your domain suffix

The name of your website is half the choice. Now you have the other half to choose...the ending, which is often called the **domain suffix**. Examples of these are .com, .org, .net

The ending of the web address is intended to indicate the purpose of the website. For instance, ".gov" indicates that it is a government website, ".org" indicates that it is an organization, ".ca" means that it is a Canadian site and ".com" indicates that it is for commercial use (this was the initial intention anyway). Particular website endings may have their own specific sets of rules for who can register using those endings. The suffix ".com" tends to be what people default to when looking up a website, so going with something familiar is not a bad idea.

Setting up your website

Now that you have a domain name, you are ready to set up your website. Your next steps will depend on the choice that you made between *Blogger, WordPress.com* and *WordPress.org*. Follow the corresponding instructions. There will likely be upgrading options along the way. Do your best to read and understand the options available to you in order to make an educated choice as to whether or not you will need the upgrades. If you need to, you can always upgrade or downgrade later on.

To set up Blogger as your website:

STEP 1

Go to www.blogger.com

STEP 2

It will then give you the option to sign in using your *Google* account information. Sign in.

Blogger is owned by *Google*, so if you have already signed up for any *Google* products (such as *Gmail* or *YouTube*), then you have a *Google* Account. Enter the email address and password which you used to set up your previous *Google* account. For example, if you have a *Gmail* account use your *Gmail* address and password to enter *Blogger*. If you do not have a *Google* account you will need to set one up. To do so, go to https://accounts.google.com/SignUp or search for instructions online on how to create a *Google* account.

Record in a safe place or memorize all of your login information.

STEP 3

Set up and design your *Blogger* blog/website.

Once you sign into *Blogger* you will be in the area where you can make all of your changes—as discussed before, this is often called the back-end. This is where the designing of your blog/website will take place, and is also where you will create your future blog posts.

Click on the "new blog" button in order to set up your blog. *Blogger* will then walk you through the setup process.

Note: Remember, if you would like to appear more professional, paying to upgrade your domain name so it does not include the name "blogger" is a good idea.

Once you set up your blog, if you click the "View Blog" button you will see what your viewers will see, which is often referred to as the **front-end**.

STEP 4

Add static pages, if desired—a static page being a web page that has information that does not change except for necessary updates (such as a *contact* page and an *about* page).

This will be done by going to the back-end of your blog. If you have viewed your blog page, it has likely opened up in a new window. To return to the back-end, simply go to the web page which has your back-end of your website opened on it. You can also get to the back-end of your *Blogger* site by clicking on the tiny *Blogger* logo (an orange square with a white capital "B" in it), typically found in the top left of your *Blogger* page, then click on the title of the blog which you would like to make changes to.

The list of blog options will be found in a column on the left hand side. From this list of options click the "Pages" button. Click the "New page" button which is probably at the top of your screen. Give your page a title and add your desired content. It is then a good idea to "Save" then "Preview" your page before publishing it.

Always click the "Save" button before leaving the page in order to prevent losing your work.

Once your page appears as desired click the orange "Publish" button—your page will not become public until you do so.

If you are to view your blog/website right now you will notice that the page you just created will not show up in the menu bar—this is because you need to add the page to it. We will do this in the next step.
STEP 5

Add your new page (such as your "about" page) to your menu bar.

From your back-end screen, click on "Layout" (likely in the column on the left hand side of your screen).

You will now see several boxes with different titles and content. Find the box which says "Pages" inside of it, then click on "Edit" within that box.

You will now see a list of "pages to show". Select the page(s) that you would like to appear on the menu bar.

Click the orange "Save" button within this window, then click the orange "Save Arrangement" button on the main back-end page.

Click on "View blog" to ensure that your additional page is now in your menu bar.
STEP 6

Be sure to logout once you are done. You will possibly find the logout button in a dropdown menu under your profile picture in the top right of your screen.

Watch the following video to see how to create a *Blogger* website:

https://youtu.be/xA9Ms6CNnaM

To set up *WordPress.com* as your website:

STEP 1

Go to www.wordpress.com

STEP 2

Click the "Create Website" button. (This button may change as *WordPress.com* upgrades, but it should remain obvious as to where to click to begin your setup process. For instance, the button may say "Get Started.")

STEP 3

WordPress.com will then walk you through the setup of your website.

Remember the suggestion of paying to upgrade your domain name if you would like for your website to not include the name "wordpress" in it.

Be sure to record in a safe place or memorize all of your login information.

STEP 4

Be sure to logout once you are done. You will possibly find the logout button in a dropdown menu under your profile picture in the top right of your screen.

Watch the following video to see how to set up a *WordPress. Com* website:

https://youtu.be/Pz__oy_YUmw

To set up *WordPress.org* as your website

Note: We are going to be spending the rest of this chapter focusing on WordPress.org.

If you are going to use *WordPress.org* for your website (a self-hosted site), you will need to first sign up with a web host provider. The web host provider is the service that will allow you to put your website on their server for a cost. You are basically renting their land so you can put your *WordPress* file on it.

Once you are signed up with a web host provider then you will need to install the *WordPress* software. Below, I will walk you through these steps.

Note: Most web host providers offer an extended service to install *WordPress* for you and get you set up. If you are limited on time or struggle with the setup process, investing in having your *WordPress.org* website set up for you is an option well worth considering.

Choosing a web host provider

There are many web host providers available. A simple internet search will give you a list of resources to check out. Some of the widely used web host providers are:

HostGator http://www.hostgator.com
GoDaddy http://www.godaddy.com/
Bluehost http://www.bluehost.com/

I use *Bluehost* and have experienced great reliability and excellent customer support from them.

It is a good idea to read up on a few different web host providers in order to understand which one would best suit your needs and budget. I highly recommend that you go with a service that is known for good customer support. There are actually real living, breathing people behind these services, so you can even call the help desk and ask questions before you sign up!

If you choose *Bluehost* as your web host provider, it would be greatly appreciated if you signed up using my affiliate link. This would in no way hinder the service which you will receive, it would simply be a kind gesture on your behalf as it would provide me with a small commission on the sale. Here is my affiliate link: http://www.bluehost.com/track/ hungryforpurpose

Signing up with a web host provider

Now that you have chosen a web host provider, go to their website (or use the affiliate link above) and follow the instructions to get started. There will likely be a "get started now" button, or some variation of those words. The start-up process will be a little different for each provider, but each one should walk you through the steps. Once you have entered all of your sign up information, you should receive a welcome email from your web host provider with your login information. Be sure to record in a safe place or memorize all of your login information and your password for your hosting account. This set of login information is for your web hosting only, you will soon have another set of login information that you will use for making changes to your actual *WordPress* website.

The video below will walk you through how to sign up with the web host provider *Bluehost*.

Note: When the video gets to the part about choosing the upgrades and options, keep in mind that you can make changes to your choices later on if need be. If you are unsure of what options are necessary for you, either a web search on your questions can be done or you can call customer service of the web host provider to ask for guidance.

In order to gain a bit more knowledge before moving forward, you can check your web host providers website for "getting started" videos and articles. There will likely be a search bar in the main tool bar to look up the getting started information. If you get stuck, simply "Google" your question. I suggest that you only get a brief overview at this point. Don't feel that you have to understand everything about your web host provider and their services, you will learn as you go through the setup process and it will become more familiar as you move forward.

Watch the following video on a web host provider purchase:

https://youtu.be/Tm01co_n37g

Now that you are signed up with a web host provider, you have land to put *WordPress* onto. In order to access your cyber land, go to your web host provider's website (eg. www.bluehost.com) and find the place to log into your account (likely a button that says "login"). Enter your domain name that you just registered, and your password. If you were to go to your website right now you will see an "empty piece of land" because you have not yet put your virtual house (*WordPress*) onto your land. That will be our next step.

Installing *WordPress* onto your web host hosting account

If you recall from the *WordPress websites* section, *WordPress* is essentially the software (the CMS—content management system) that you are going to use to build your website. Installing your CMS is similar to installing software onto your computer. This may sound a bit complicated, but it is fairly straightforward. Without *WordPress* (or another CMS), you basically have empty land that needs a house on it. *WordPress* will be like your house.

Some web host providers may automatically have *WordPress* installed. You can check whether or not WordPress is on your website by opening a new internet window, and then typing your website address into the web browser. If *WordPress* is installed you will see some sort of message welcoming you to a *WordPress* site. Otherwise, you will likely see the logo of your web host provider somewhere on your website.

If you went with *Bluehost* as your web host provider then you *will* need to install *WordPress*.

Because I use *Bluehost* as my hosting provider, I will walk you through the steps for this particular provider. There will likely be step by step tutorials for installing *WordPress* onto the hosting account on the web host provider's website that you choose. You can also search for tutorials by typing into a search engine, something like this: "how to install *WordPress* onto your [web host provider name] hosting account."

Instructions for installing WordPress onto your *Bluehost* hosting account:

STEP 1

Go to *Bluehost* at www.bluehost.com and click on login (likely in the top right of the upper menu bar) and enter your login information. You would have had to already gone through the signup process in order to be able to do this step.

STEP 2

You will now be on your Control Panel (C Panel for short).

STEP 3

Go to the website section. This section should have a title such as "website builders."

STEP 4

Click the icon "Install *WordPress*."

You will now likely have the option to either do it yourself for free, or pay to have *WordPress* installed onto your website for you. As mentioned earlier, if you are short on time or are challenged with the technology side of things, having this done for you is an option well worth considering. Included in the paid service is having a *WordPress theme* installed for you also. You will be learning about *themes* shortly—a **theme** is basically a template for your website. You will be learning how to install a theme onto your website very soon.

If you have chosen to install *WordPress* yourself, you will find a button to click labeled "Install".

You will now be prompted to choose which of your domain names you want to install *WordPress* onto. If you are just starting out, you likely only have one domain name to choose from.

STEP 5

As *WordPress* is installing, and you wait for it to load, you can look at themes for purchase. There will also be many free themes to choose from, we will cover this in the next section. Themes are basic templates that you will use to create the look and function for your website.

STEP 6

Once *WordPress* loads, check your email for your *WordPress* login info (this will be the email address that you used to register your web host provider/hosting account). Record this information in a secure place. This login info will only be available for a short while (approx. 12 hours) for security purposes so retrieve it immediately.

The "URL" is your web address.

Your "**admin URL**" is the URL that you will need to type into the web browser in order to access the administration end of your website in order to make changes to your website and post new content. Your admin URL will look something like this: www.(yourname).com/wp-admin

Your username will be required to log into *WordPress*.

To retrieve your password, click "view" beside the red "credential" button. You can change this password later if you desire.

I know I have said this many times already, but be sure to record in a safe place or memorize all of your login information. There is not many things more frustrating than being unable to access online services due to not knowing the password.

You will have separate login information for your web host account and *WordPress*. Don't be confused with the two sets of information. It is as if you now have a key to the gate of your property (your web host provider login info), and a key to your house (*WordPress* login info).

Be sure to logout of your hosting account once you are done working with it.

Note: After *WordPress* is installed, you likely *will not* need to access your web host provider too often. Most of your website changes will be made through *WordPress*; therefore it will be your *WordPress* login info that you will be using most often. If you would like to set up an email address that is specific to your website (eg. yourname@websitename. com), this is done through your web host provider: in order to do so, log into your web hosting account and do a search for instructions on how to set up an email account.

Watch the following video to see how to install *WordPress* onto your *BlueHost* hosting account:

https://youtu.be/fbBXGJtmXHo

Congratulations! You now have a self-hosted website!

c) Developing Your Website

Another note: Be sure to always logout of your *WordPress* site (or any of your online accounts) when you have completed making changes on your administrative end. You will likely find the logout button in a dropdown menu under your profile picture in the top right of your screen.

Remember that we are only talking about *WordPress.org* for the rest of this chapter.

A website is essentially empty when you first install it. If you type your website address into the web browser, at this point, it will not look like much. It is like purchasing a new house; it is typically unfurnished and the walls are white. The CMS (*WordPress*) which you installed previously will allow you to "decorate" by adding content (a blog, web pages, videos etc.).

This is where the fun begins. Let's start shaping your website into something that is functional.

You will need to begin by going into the back-end of your website (this may also be referred to as the administrative end). Type in your admin URL that you were given during your *WordPress* installation process, then enter your username and password into the appropriate spots. Your admin URL will look something like this: [www.(yourname).com/wp-admin]. Be sure to use your login information for *WordPress* and not get it confused with your login information for your web hosting account.

You should now be on what *WordPress* calls the *Dashboard*. The **dashboard** is the screen where you will make all your changes and add content.

To learn more about *WordPress,* find the small *WordPress* icon, likely in the very top left of your dashboard. Hover over that icon with your mouse and you will get a dropdown menu with some options such as "About WordPress" and "Documentation." There should be a link to the *WordPress* forums on the dropdown menu as well. You can read through the getting started articles and flip through the documentation in order to gain familiarity with *WordPress* and learn where you can get more information if you get stuck on something.

Choosing a theme

The best place to start when setting up your website is to choose a theme. A theme is basically a template, and is what gives your website a specific look and feel to the presentation of your content. The theme lays out the *basic* website design and function, with room for customizing the colour, graphics, layout and more.

One way to choose a theme is to first sketch out what you envision your website to look like, and then match it as close as possible to an available theme. Another way, probably the easiest way, is to go through the available themes and find one you like.

With some themes you will be able to make more changes than others, depending on what was coded into it. For instance, some will allow you to make changes to fonts, and some will not. You will learn what you can and cannot do as you work with the themes. We are going to be focusing mainly on the basic setup of your website. The more you work with it, the more familiar you will become with how to make changes.

Each theme will have a description of its basic functions and features. It will be the easiest on you to choose one which includes the functions which you plan to have in your website. For instance, if you plan to blog as the main purpose of your website, you can choose a theme that emphasizes blogging—a blog page may also be called a posting page (most, if not all, *WordPress* themes have blogging capabilities because it was first set up as a blogging platform). If you plan on using social media such as *Facebook* and *Twitter*, ensure that your theme has buttons to link to social media sites. It is possible to add many of these options later on, but it will be less of a headache if you plan ahead. Also, it is a very good idea to pay attention to whether or not the theme is compatible with all devices (such as iPhones, Android phones, tablets and desktops). In the theme description, it may be described as **mobile responsive**. This means that the website has been designed for optimal viewing, navigating and interacting on mobile devices. A very large percentage of viewers are searching the web with mobile devices so you want to ensure that your website will appear correctly no matter how it is viewed. Most *WordPress* themes are now mobile responsive.

It is inevitable that you will make changes to your website as you grow with your online platform. At this moment, you are simply getting an online presence so you can get onto the field and into the game.

How to install a theme on your *WordPress.org* site:

STEP 1

Log into your *WordPress* dashboard (the back-end of your website), by entering your login URL and password.

STEP 2

Hover over "Appearance" in the menu, which is likely on the far left side of your screen.

STEP 3

From the "Appearance" pop-out menu, Click "Themes." You will now be on your themes page.

STEP 4

Navigate through the available themes in order to find one that will be suitable for your website. You may find a button labeled "Add New" which will give you various categories of themes to choose from, such as "featured", "popular" and "latest."

We will be checking out the free themes. There are paid ones to choose from as well if you find that none of the free ones suit your needs. There are, however, many free ones to choose from so that is a great place to start.

STEP 5

Scan through the themes. Once you come across one that catches your eye, click on it to enlarge it. What you see will be the home page, which will be the first page that the viewer would see when visiting your website. Scroll down to see the entire website. The most important part of each web page is the part that people will see before scrolling down; this part of the web page is called *above the fold*. What the viewer sees will vary depending on what device they are looking at your website with (phone, tablet, computer, etc.). You could always view the website from different devices to see what it would look like.

To exit out of viewing a particular theme, click the X on the top left of the theme description and you will be taken back to the theme choices.

Look for a theme that has a basic layout that resonates with you— but you do not have to pay attention to minor details like colours and graphics because you will eventually make changes to many of the features. You will also add pages, pictures, logos and many other modifications once your theme is installed. The theme that you choose will simply be your starting point.

STEP 6

Read the description of the theme, which will likely appear on the left hand side of your screen once you have clicked on a theme.

The theme name will be at the top of the theme description. The designer name will be written under the theme name. It is a good idea to do an internet search on the designer to ensure that they are reputable. Just ensure that there are no red flags, such as several poor reviews on a specific web designer. You can also check the star ratings. Some of the newer themes may not have any ratings yet so this may not help you.

As you come across themes that may work for you, write them down. Continue going through the many themes until you find several that you like, then go back and narrow it down to one.

Once you have the theme that looks like *The One*, click the "Install" button. After the theme is installed you MUST click "activate" in order to make it usable.

The step of choosing a theme may become overwhelming as there are so many options; and it can be challenging to match the website to your vision. Take your time to look through different themes. This is a process that you will not want to rush. You may want to do this over a few sittings.

If you find that you do not like the theme that you chose, you can install another one. Just keep in mind that once you make a lot of changes to your website and start adding content, all of your changes may not transfer over. It is best to experiment with different themes before you add all of your content.

The video tutorial in the next section begins with walking you through the process of choosing and installing a theme.

d) Designing Your Website

Note: This section continues to pertain to *WordPress.org*

It would be impossible and overwhelming to go over everything about designing a website. And, the options available for your website design will depend on the theme that you chose and your comfort level with the technologies available. So we will just touch on the basics in order to get you going. This will be one of those things that you will continue to learn as you go. So let's get started.

There are a ton of tutorials and documentation at www.wordpress. org that you can check out as you continue to develop your *WordPress. org* website.

You certainly have the option of paying a web designer to build your website for you, but you are still better off being a little educated on what you want before you pay someone to try and figure it out for you. Even if you are not the one who will be doing all of the back-end work, it is a good idea to understand a bit of what goes on behind the scenes of your website. Like owning a car, you don't need to know how to rebuild the engine, but it is a good thing to know how to check the oil and fill the windshield washer fluid.

Check out this video for an introduction on how to design your *WordPress.org* website. This video also includes how to install a theme onto your website.

https://youtu.be/XxD3yAYazRI

Adding content to your web pages

Web pages are the individual pages within a website. A website can contain many web pages such as: an about page, a blog page, a contact page and so on. Web pages can be used to display a variety of information such as upcoming events, resources, books and other items for sale, and much more. These pages can be static pages or a blog page. Remember that a static page is one that the information generally stays the same. A blog page is one that has the ability to have new material constantly added to it—referred to as posts.

Some of the following steps may vary depending on the theme that you choose.

Steps for adding content to your web pages:

STEP 1

Log into your *WordPress* dashboard using your *WordPress* admin URL and password.

STEP 2

Hover over "Pages" on the menu (likely on the left hand side of your dashboard), then click from the pop-out menu either "Add new" in order to add a new page, or "All Pages" to make changes to an existing page.

STEP 3

If you are adding a new page, name the page in the title bar then enter your desired content into the content box below the title bar. There will be two tabs on the top right corner of this box: "Visual" and "Text." If you are adding plain text you can enter it into the "Visual" box which will make it easier to visualize what your content will look like. If you are adding any code (for videos etc.) you will need to switch to the "Text" box and enter it in there.

STEP 4

If you are making changes to an existing page, hover over the page name that you wish to make changes to in the list of pages. Click "edit" under the page title. Type, or copy and paste your content into the content box.

STEP 5

CLICK the "UPDATE" button to save your updated content, or the "Publish" button to publish new content. Your content will NOT be saved if you do not do this step.

STEP 6

Take a look at your site to see what it will look like to the viewer. You can do this by hovering over your website name in the very top left corner of your dashboard. Then from the dropdown menu, click "visit site."

Note: If you added a new page, depending on the theme that you are using, it may not yet show up in your menu bar. You might have to go to "menus" in the pop-out menu of "Appearance" to add that new page to your menu. I will show you how to do this in the following video on adding pages to your website.

At this point, you can play around with the website a bit in order to learn how to make changes to it. You will continue to learn as you go along. Don't worry, you will not need to know *everything* about the website in order to get started.

You will figure out in a hurry if you will be able to work with the theme that you choose. If you find that the theme is difficult to work with or if it is just not working with the vision that you have, you can try another one by repeating the steps in the *Installing a theme* section in this chapter. When you switch from one theme to another, your content may or may not transfer, depending on the content and the website capabilities. It is a good idea to create all of your written content in a word document (or another word processor document), then copy and paste it into your website. This will provide you with a backup of your content.

Once you find the theme that you are going to stick with you can get a bit more serious in your website designing efforts. It will take practice and trial and error to figure things out. Website building is likely a new thing to you, so you are going to need to apply patience and perseverance.

You will have options to upload items such as banners and logos to your website. These are items that you can have made for you by a graphic arts designer or you can be creative and make graphics yourself through software such as *Photoshop*. When you are satisfied with the basic aesthetics of your website, you can further develop your pages by adding content to them.

Congratulations! You now have a functioning website. Your website will evolve over time as you figure things out and add content, but this is a great start.

Watch this video to learn how to add web pages to your website, and add content to your web pages.

https://youtu.be/Aftq7iYra7Y

Check out the sample website that we will be working on throughout this book, in order to give you an idea of what you are working towards: http://www.encouragingcontribution.com/demo1

We are focusing on a basic website setup in order to get you started. Know that there are many options for your website, but don't get distracted by all of the possibilities. Start with the basics, then continue moving forward and you will grow in your ability to use your website to its potential.

CHAPTER 6

Plank 2: Blog

A **blog** is typically a web page which frequently has new content added to it—similar to a journal. A blog is a popular way to share content on a continual basis, and can be an effective tool to promote ones works and get your name out there. Each new entry to a blog is called a **blog post**. Each time a new post is made, the previous ones will remain sequentially available under the newer posts. The old posts may also be categorized and tagged with keywords so your readers can easily find the ones they are interested in. The most effective blogs tend to stick to a theme or topic, targets a specific audience, serves a purpose for getting the information out, and promotes the writer as a reputable source for this information.

Hobbyists can blog about their craft, authors can blog about particular matters or story characters, and experts can blog about their expertise. The opportunities for blogging are endless. If you have a message that is deeply engraved on your heart and aches to be shared with others, then that will likely be the focus of your discussions.

The three website building tools which we have looked at (*Blogger*, *WordPress.com* and *WordPress.org*) can also be used for blogging. By default there is likely a blog page on the website, which you have set up in the last chapter, so to begin blogging is fairly straightforward. A blog page (remember this may also be called a posting page) will be the page that you can add posts to.

Note: Once you have a blog set up, there will be opportunities for comments from readers. This is an excellent way to engage with your followers. Unfortunately though, some comments may not be legitimate as they may be spam or phishing emails. A phishing email is a fraudulent email that is legitimate-looking but it attempts to gather personal information. There are spam filters and other security features that assist in protecting you from those types of activities, but it will depend on what you have in place—you may need to make some modifications. Security features and spam filters are not topics that we are going to go into in this book. However, you should be aware of the issues of spam and phishing emails, and educate yourself on methods of protecting yourself from them. When approving blog comments and engaging in correspondence, use discretion and discernment.

a) Blogging with *Blogger*

If you recall from earlier in this book, *Blogger* by default is a single blogging page so you can use this purely as a blogging tool if you wish. If you used *Blogger* to build your website then you would have added static pages to it.

If you wish to blog about any kind of journey, art or skill purely as a hobby...or if you intend for your content to primarily be for friends and family (perhaps journaling about your kids growing up, sharing vacation photos, or teaching scrapbooking techniques), then a free single page blog is what would likely be the best choice. This is the easiest to set up, get started, and maintain. In these cases, marketing will likely not be a major focus because you are not looking for followers and customers because you already have your intended audience.

Blogger is not limited to hobbyists though. It has been used by authors, other artists, and business owners as their main online information station. Just remember that this type of blog can be limiting to its marketing potential. You can review the pros and cons of *Blogger* in chapter 5 section a).

Blogger can also be a handy tool for blogging about a specific event like a conference or a family reunion. In this case it would be used for a period of time, but may not be used on an ongoing basis.

To start blogging with Blogger:

STEP 1

Log into your *Blogger* account.

If you have not yet set up a *Blogger* account see the instructions on how to do so in Chapter 5 section b) under the heading: *To set up Blogger as your website.*

STEP 2

Add a post by clicking the orange button that is to the right of your blog title. This button has a picture of a pencil on it, and if you hover over it, it will display the label "create new post."

STEP 3

Type in the desired title for your post into the text box that has the words *Post title*. Add your content into the large text box in the middle of your screen.

STEP 4

It is a good idea to save, then preview your blog post before you make it public. To do this, click the "save" button in the top right hand corner of your screen. Then click the "Preview" button to see what your post will look like. Make any necessary changes. Once you are satisfied with your blog post carry onto the next step.

STEP 5

Click the orange "Publish" button.

Note: From the "Post Settings" menu bar on your posting page (likely found on the right of the text box), you can explore additional options such as scheduling your post for a later time and date.

There you go! You have created your first blog post!

STEP 6

Be sure to logout once you are done. You will probably find the log-out button in a dropdown menu under your profile picture in the top right of your screen.

b) Blogging with *WordPress.com*

After you have set up and designed your website:
STEP 1

Log into your *Wordpress.com* website using your login information.
STEP 2

Go to your dashboard.

You are likely on a page that summarizes your WordPress.com website(s). To access the dashboard for your website you will need to click on the option (likely in a menu on the left hand side) that will be labeled something like "dashboard" or "WP Admin."
STEP 3

Once you are on your dashboard, hover over "Posts" in the left hand column, then click "Add New" from the pop-out menu.

Type your title into the title bar, then type (or copy and paste) your content into the space below.

With this content box, you can switch between "Visual" or "Text"— these buttons are found on the top right of the content box. If you are adding plain text you can use either the "Visual" or "Text" box. If you are adding any code (programming language) or a link to a video, it will need to be placed in the "text" box.
STEP 4

Click the "Save Draft" button.
STEP 5

Click "Preview" to take a look at your post before you make it public.

Return to the dashboard by hovering over "My Sites" (or possibly a slightly different label) in the top left corner, then click on "WP Admin" from the dropdown menu.

The post which you are working on will be found by hovering over "Posts" in the left menu bar of the dashboard. Then click on "All Posts" from the pop-out menu. You will then see the Draft of the post which you are working on. Hover over that post then click on "Edit" from the menu. Continue to make changes to your post until you are satisfied with it.
STEP 6

Once you are satisfied with your post, click "Publish" from the Post Editing page.

Voila! You have made a blog post!
STEP 7

Be sure to logout of your site once you are all done. You will likely find the logout button in a dropdown menu possibly under your profile picture in the top right of your screen.

Note: The back-end (referred to as the Dashboard) of *Wordpress.com* and *Wordpress.org* are quite similar. Watch the video in the following "Blogging with *WordPress.org*" section to gain greater understanding of how to create blog posts using *WordPress*.

c) Blogging with *WordPress.org*

The third option is blogging with *WordPress.org*. If you went with this option and you have your website set up, you will most likely have a blog page in place on your website. If you need to set up a *WordPress.org* website, see the instruction on how to do so in chapter 5 section b)

To begin blogging with *WordPress.org:*
STEP 1

Log in with your *Wordpress.org* admin URL.
STEP 2

From the dashboard, go to "posts" on the side menu bar and click on "add new" from the pop-out menu.

STEP 3

Type into the title bar what you would like your post to be called.

STEP 4

Type in your content (or copy and paste) into the content box below the title bar.

With this content box, you can switch between "Visual" or "Text"— these buttons are found on the top right of the content box. If you are adding plain text you can use either the "Visual" or "Text" box. If you are adding any code (programming language) or a link to a video, it will need to be placed in the "text" box.

STEP 5

To add a picture, click the "add media" button then upload your photo.

STEP 6

If you desire to add a video, simply copy the URL for the video then paste it into the "text" box in the desired position within your post.

STEP 7

Click the blue "Publish" button to publish your post immediately, or schedule your post for a later date. To schedule your post, click "edit" beside "Publish immediately" in the publish task bar (likely on the right side of the screen), then select the date and time that you would like your post to be published. Click "OK" then click the "Schedule" button. You could also choose "Save Draft" if you would like to continue working on this post at a later time. This is a very important step, as your blog will NOT save changes if you do not click "Publish", "Schedule" or "Save Draft."

STEP 8

View your site to ensure that your blog has posted, or you can "Preview" the post if you have scheduled it for a later date.

STEP 9

Be sure to logout once you are done. You will probably find the logout button in a dropdown menu under your profile picture in the top right of your screen.

Watch this video on adding a blog post to a *Wordpress.org* blog.

https://youtu.be/odieMviyUEE

Note: You may find that *WordPress* has made some changes since the publishing of this video. *WordPress* works hard to improve their user's experience, so any changes that have been made are hopefully straight forward.

CHAPTER 7

Plank 3: Opt-In Boxes

a) What is an Opt-In Box?

An **Opt-In Box** is a box on a web page where you enter your name and email in exchange for something. An Opt-in box may also be called a *sign up form.* You may be opting-in to receive a digital product like an ebook, or a video. Or, you may be opting-in to receive a newsletter or other recurring information like a blog. When you enter your name into an opt-in box, it is then put on a list—appropriately named an **email list.** The person or company that you sign up with owns that list and can now use it to market further products and services to you and the other email addresses that are on that list. An email address is like gold in the web world. If you are looking to monetize (make money) from your website, one way to do this is by **email marketing:** selling or presenting to your email list. I have to admit, email marketing sounds a little sleazy…pelting people's inboxes with pleas for them to read and buy your "stuff" makes me a little squeamish. Email marketing *can* be "sleazy," but it does not need to be. And I certainly do not encourage it to be.

I am teaching *purpose,* so I'm specifically talking about ways to purposefully connect with those who are intended to hear what you have to offer—whether it is a product, written work or a service. If you have a message that you believe in and are passionate about sharing with others, then you need a way of connecting and communicating with your audience. One of the most practical ways to do this is by email; in order to do this you will need to sign up with an *email marketing service*, which you will learn about in the next section.

Note: At the time of this publication, it is not possible to place a sign-up form directly onto a *WordPress.com* site. The opt-in boxes which are created through an email service works most easily with a self-hosted website; therefore, we will only be working with *WordPress.org* websites in this chapter.

b) What is an Email Marketing Service?

An **email marketing service** offers an online system that collects and manages emails. This service is often referred to as an **autoresponder** because it can deliver a series of messages automatically. This is where it really pays off to have a self-hosted site, since email marketing can most easily be used with such a site.

There are many email marketing services. Doing a simple web search on this will bring up numerous options. Check out the various email marketing providers, as well as some reviews, before making a choice. Ensure that whichever service you choose has tutorials available on how to use their system. Going with the most popular choice isn't guaranteed to be the best, but if lots of people are using it then there will be a lot of information online which will make your learning process a little easier.

I use the service *AWeber* for my email marketing. They charge a monthly fee around the $20 mark. The following videos and tutorials within this chapter will walk you through the basics of email marketing using *AWeber*.

The email marketing service *MailChimp* is also widely used. At the time of this publication, *MailChimp* is free up to a certain amount of subscribers, then they charge for lists that grow over a particular number.

c) Sign Up With an Email Marketing Service

To sign up with an email marketing service, go to your chosen provider's website (such as *AWeber* or *MailChimp*) and follow their signup instructions. There should be "getting started" instructions available, which is a great place to begin learning how to use this tool.

If you chose to go with *AWeber*, I would be greatly appreciative if you use my affiliate link to sign up for this service: http://www.aweber. com/?425455 (using this link will not interfere with your service, it will simply bless me with a commission on the sale).

Note: Be informed that there is a law in place that regulates commercial emails, therefore you are required to provide a valid physical postal address or P.O. box address which will be included at the bottom of your emails. This must be a valid mailing address where you can receive postal mail. Some options are to use your business address or obtain a P.O. box.

d) Setting Up a List

The first thing you will need to do after signing up with an email marketing service is start a list. A list is where the email addresses and names will be stored; you can make different email lists for different content. One person may only want to sign up for a blog whereas someone else may want to only sign up for a free report; therefore, their names and email addresses would go onto different lists. You will then be able to segregate which content you would like to send to specific lists.

Here is how you create a list in AWeber:

STEP 1

Log into your *AWeber* account.

If you have gone through a different email marketing service the steps may be similar, depending on the provider. You will likely find tutorials online or on your chosen provider's website.

STEP 2

From your *AWeber* page, click on "Manage lists" in the top menu bar.

STEP 3

Click the large green button labelled "Create A List."

STEP 4

Fill in all of the appropriate information then go to the "next step."

STEP 5

Fill in the next set of information (list name and description) then go to the "next step."

STEP 6

Make any desired changes to your confirmation message then click at the bottom of the screen "Approve Message & Create List."

You will then be brought to your account overview page. At the top of this screen there are the words "Current List:" with a dropdown menu beside it. If you click the dropdown menu this will show you all of your current lists. If you would like to make changes to one specific list, click on "Manage List" in the top tool bar, then click on the list which you would like to make changes to.

Note: When you are done working in your AWeber account, be sure to logout.

Watch the following video to see how to create a list using *AWeber*:

https://youtu.be/iJ-TUw9XqIw

e) Create and Install an Opt-In Box On a Static Page

You now have a list through your email marketing provider. Now you need a *way* for people to sign up to that list. This is where opt-in boxes come in. Remember that opt-in boxes are often referred to as a sign up form; these two terms are the same thing.

You can also install an opt-in box/sign-up-form for your blog, but the steps for that are a bit different. We will start with installing a Sign Up form onto a static page. After this, you will learn how people can sign up for your blog.

To create an opt-in box through AWeber and install it on a static page, follow these steps:

STEP 1

From your *AWeber* home page, click on the dropdown menu beside "Current List:" (near the top of the page). Click on the list from this dropdown menu that you would like to create an opt-in box for.

Note: It is very important that you select the desired list or you will end up having people sign up for the incorrect content. It is a good idea to always double check that you are on the correct list when making changes within your email marketing service.

STEP 2

Click on the menu item "Sign Up Forms" near the top of your screen.

Remember that a sign up form and an opt-in box are the same thing.

STEP 3

Click the button "Create Your First Sign Up Form."

STEP 4

Choose a template for your sign up form. Click "Load Template."

STEP 5

Customize the template by clicking on the desired "edit" areas (header, text boxes etc.).

STEP 6

Click "Save Your Form" then click the button to go to the next step.

STEP 7

Name your form on this *Basic Settings* page. You can select different options here for your *Thank You Page* and your *Already Subscribed* Page.

STEP 8

Click "Save Your Form" then click the button to go to the next step.

STEP 9

To install your own form, click "I Will Install My Form."

STEP 10

You will now see a text box with some code in it. Click on the code and highlight all of it, then right click on the highlighted text, then "copy".

STEP 11

Log into your *WordPress.org* website using your login URL.

STEP 12

From your dashboard, click on "Pages", then click on "All Pages" from the pop-out menu. Click "edit" under the title of the page which you would like to install your sign up form on.

If you want to install your sign up form on a page which you have not yet created, do that now. Follow the instructions in Chapter 5 section d) to create an additional web page.

STEP 13

Ensure that the "text" content box is up front. Place your curser within the text box on the desired position of where you would like to put your sign up form. Right click, then hit paste. The code which you copied for your sign up form should now appear in the text box.

STEP 14

Click the "Update" button (this will likely be a blue button).

STEP 15

Visit your site to see how the sign up form appears.

To visit your site hover over your website title in the top left corner of your Dashboard then click "Visit Site" from the dropdown menu.

STEP 16

It is a good idea to sign up to your own list to ensure that your opt-in box is working.

Watch the following video to see how to put an opt-in box on a static page using *AWeber*:

https://youtu.be/E3ZefJAdqVo

You now have your email marketing service in place! I suspect that you will want to attract an audience to your works. We will not be covering audience building in this book because we are focusing on the mechanics of getting you all set up; although, there is a ton of information available on how to grow your audience. I encourage you to continue your learning process on how to utilize your email marketing tool to its fullest potential.

f) Enable People to Sign Up For Your Blog

The steps for creating a way for people to sign up to receive your blog automatically is a bit different than the steps for allowing people to sign up for content from a static page. The reason why the steps are a bit different is because your blog constantly has material added to it. Every time you make a post you want it to be sent to the list of people who have signed up for it; therefore you need to connect your blog and the email list. In *AWeber* this is done through what they call a **Blog Broadcast**. Other email marketing services may have a different term for this.

This may sound a bit confusing, but stick with me. Not to worry if you don't understand this completely; you just need to know that in order for your blog to be sent to the people who sign up for it, you need to connect your blog to your email marketing list—*AWeber* calls this connection a *Blog Broadcast*.

Here are the steps to create a Blog Broadcast in AWeber:

STEP 1

Log into your *AWeber* account.

STEP 2

Create a list for your blog by following the steps in section d) *Setting up a list*.

STEP 3

On your *AWeber* home page, ensure that the list name for your blog which you just created appears in the box that is beside the words *Current List:* (This box is at the top of the screen).

STEP 4

Go to the "messages" tab and from the dropdown menu click on "Blog Broadcasts."

STEP 5

Click the button "Create A Blog Broadcast."

STEP 6

Fill in your RSS Feed URL. This will likely be your full website URL with "*/feed/*" tacked onto the end. So it will look something like this: http://www.yourwebsite.com/feed/

There may be a video within *AWeber* on creating Blog Broadcasts that shows where you can find this information. It can be tricky to find your URL for your RSS feed, so if you get stuck on this step you can reference the provided documentation within *Wordpress*, or contact the *AWeber* customer support team.

Note: RSS stands for Really Simple Syndication; it is used for delivering frequently changing web content such as a blog. It is the RSS Feed that allows the blog to connect with your email list and therefore enables the posts to be sent out to your list each time a new post is made.

STEP 7

Choose a template from the templates list. You can choose the "plain" template if you like, but you MUST choose a template in order for it to know where to pull your information from. Click "Load Template."

At the bottom of the web page which you are on, you should see a few options that you can choose from. Make changes to these options if you like. If you would like your blog posts to be sent out as soon as you publish them, make sure that the "send automatically" box is checked off, otherwise you will need to approve each one individually before they are sent out.

STEP 8

Click "Save Blog Broadcast."

g) Install an Opt-In Box for Your Blog onto Your Blog Page

STEP 1

Create a sign up form for your blog page.

First, ensure that the list that you made for your blog is selected in the *Current List.*

Follow the steps in section e) *Create and install an opt-in box on a static page* up until the end of STEP 9.

STEP 2

Log into your *WordPress.org* website Dashboard.

STEP 3

Hover over "Pages" in your sidebar, then click on "All Pages" from the pop-out menu.

STEP 4

Click on "Edit" under your Blog page.

STEP 5

You can install the code for the sign up form here in your text box, similar to how it was done for the static page (section e in this chapter); however, the opt-in box will then appear in your list of blog posts and will not be easily seen. Installing your opt-in box on the side will be much more effective.

To install your form so it appears on the side of your blog page, install it into a text box widget. To do this, hover over "Appearance" in your sidebar, then click on "Widgets" on the pop-out menu.

STEP 6

If there is a box labeled "Text" in the Sidebar list, click on the drop-down arrow to reveal an area where you can enter text.

If there is not a box labeled "Text" in the Sidebar list, find the box labeled "Text" in the list of available widgets. Click this text box then drag and drop it into your sidebar list. Click on the dropdown arrow of this text box to reveal an area where you can enter text.

STEP 7

Go back to your *AWeber* page. Click on the block of code to highlight it. Right click on it, then click "copy."

STEP 8

Go back to your *WordPress* page. Click inside the text area of the text box. Right click. Click "paste."

STEP 9

Click the "save" button.

STEP 10

Visit your site then go to your blog page and ensure that the opt-in box appears on the side of the page. If it has not, go back to your dashboard and make sure that you pressed save. If it still does not appear, there may be some variations to this step depending on your theme. You may need to experiment a bit here. I will explain this further in the tutorial video at the end of this section.

STEP 11

You can put your own name and email into your opt-in box in order to test it. Once you have confirmed your subscription to your list, go to your *WordPress.org* Dashboard.

You will need to make a blog post in order to test if your blog broadcast is working. To make a blog post, follow the steps in Chapter 6, section c) *Blogging with WordPress.org.*

Note: Any changes made to your email marketing, such as template changes, can take up to 24 hours to go through. Blog posts can also take up to three hours to show up in your inbox; therefore, you may not receive your posts immediately.

Watch the following video to see how to create a Blog Broadcast using *AWeber*:

https://youtu.be/t510pBqYHWc

h) Creating Broadcasts

A likely reason why you want a list of followers is so you can communicate with them. There are several ways in which you can do this; we already explored how you can share your blog with your list of readers through a blog broadcast. Now you will learn how to send out messages to your lists. A message that is sent out to a particular list through your email marketing service is simply called a **broadcast**. Broadcasts can be sent out immediately, or you can schedule them to be sent out at later dates and times.

Here are the steps on how to create a broadcast:
STEP 1

Sign into your *AWeber* account. Ensure that the list which you desire to send your broadcast (message) to is in the "Current List:" box.

STEP 2

Hover over "Messages" on the top menu bar. Click "Broadcasts" from the dropdown menu.

STEP 3

Click the large button labeled "Create A Broadcast" (this will likely be a green button).

Note: As *AWeber* updates their site, you may see some additional options here.

STEP 4

Type your subject into the subject line. Choose a template to enter your message into, or you can use the blank canvas if you prefer. Enter all of the information which you would like to include in this broadcast (text, images, video etc.).

STEP 5

Click "Save" then click "Next" at the bottom of your screen.

STEP 6

You will then be brought to a *Sharing* page. You can do some reading and exploring here to see how to use these options, or you can pass through this step for now.

Click "Next."

STEP 7

Here you can schedule your broadcast to go out at a later date and time if you would like.

It is a good idea to double check that you have selected your desired list to send this message to. The "Current List:" box at the top of your screen should be displaying your desired list.

Click "Save Message."

STEP 8

You will now see the title of the message which you just created under the heading *Drafts.* Here you can edit it, send yourself a test, delete it, copy it, schedule it or send it now.

Watch the following video to see how to create an *AWeber* Broadcast:

https://youtu.be/zrabCcTxClc

For an example of how you can use broadcasts, I invite you to sign up on my home page to receive *Crumbs of Purpose*, which are mini inspirations that I send out every few days: http://www.hungryforpurpose.com

i) Creating a Follow Up Series

A **follow up series** is a sequence of messages which are sent out to a particular list through your email marketing service. This is often referred to as an email campaign (also called email marketing or auto-responding). This series of emails is set up to be sent out automatically, and are triggered when the person signs up to that particular list. The purpose of these emails can vary greatly. They may be used to promote a particular product or service. They may be a sequence of information, like mini courses or tutorials, or they may be a gradual introduction to who you are and what you have to offer. There is much room for exploring the potential of a follow up series.

Follow these instructions to create a follow up series using AWeber:

STEP 1

Log into your *AWeber* account.

STEP 2

Set up a list for who you will want this email series to go to. Follow the instructions in section *d) Setting up a list.*

STEP 3

Set up an opt-in box for this list. Follow the instructions in section *e) Create and Install an Opt-In Box On a Static Page.*

Install this sign up form on the appropriate web page.

STEP 4

From the home page of your *AWeber* account, click on the "Messages" tab, then click on "Follow Up Series" from the dropdown menu.

STEP 5

Click the "Create a Follow Up" button. Once again, there may be additional options to choose from here, and the title of this action button may have changed since the publication of this book. The button which you are to click will likely be indicated with the colour green.

STEP 6

Type your subject into the subject line. Enter your content into the content area which is below the subject. You can choose a template by clicking the "templates" button or you can type directly into the content area. Your content may be straight text, or you can experiment with a mix of content; you can paste URL's from videos, or you can insert pictures or PDF's of workbooks, lessons and more. Click the "Attach Files" button to attach a file from your hard drive.

This will be the first email in this series. You will be able to create as many emails following this one as you would like.

STEP 7

Click "Save" then "Next" on the bottom right of your screen.

STEP 8

On the next screen, click "Save & Exit."

STEP 9

You will now see a box with *#1* and the title of this message that you just created. You are now ready to create the next email in this series.

STEP 10

When you are ready to create another email in this series, click the "Create A Follow Up" button.

STEP 11

Enter your subject and content for this message.

STEP 12

Click "Save" then "Next" on the bottom right of your screen.

STEP 13

You will now see *Settings* near the top of your screen; under this you will see the word *Interval* with a small box by it where you can enter the amount of days which you would like this email to be sent out after the previous message was sent.

STEP 14

Click "Save & Exit."

STEP 15

You will now see a box with the title of the message which you just created as the next email in this series.

Follow *STEP 10 to STEP 15* for as many emails as you would like in this series.

STEP 16

You can send a test for each email in order to preview the message. Make any necessary changes.

Watch the following video to see how to create a follow up series using *AWeber*:

https://youtu.be/TtRO4TfQcsw

For an example of how to use a follow up series, I invite you to sign up at http://www.hungryforpurpose.com/ya-but-how-follow-up-series/ to receive the sequence of 3 short videos "3 solutions for purposeful living." This is the same series that we just set up in the previous tutorial video.

Note: Not all subscribers to your lists are going to be legitimate. Unfortunately there is a lot of spamming and malicious activity taking place online. There are spam filters, double opt-in's and other security features that assist in protecting you from those types of activities. Security features and spam filters are not topics that we are going to go into in this book. You should be aware of these issues though, and educate yourself on this subject. Keep in mind that there are millions of websites for web surfers to choose from, so if there has been little marketing effort put in, it isn't typical to have numerous sign-ups right off the bat. If you receive many signups right away, it is a good idea to look into what you have in place for spam filters in order to ensure that the signups which you are receiving are legitimate.

CHAPTER 8

Plank 4: Social Media

Oh boy! Social media is a HUGE topic. **Social media** are online channels that are used to socially interact within virtual communities. These may also be referred to as *Social Networks*. *Social networking* is the act of connecting with people through social media. Some examples of these are *Facebook, Twitter, LinkedIn* and *Pinterest.*

Social media can be an effective way to reach out and grow your platform. There are oodles of avenues which you could take, but you cannot possibly go down every one of them…you will definitely get lost if you try to.

In order to use social media well, become proficient in a select few rather than learning a little about many. The method which will likely grant you the greatest headway is to first choose ONE. Learn it. Get good at it. Use it consistently. Then grow by choosing another avenue that seems appropriate, then repeat these steps until you are comfortable with your social media outlets. If, after giving a particular social media platform an honest try, you discover that it may not be the best choice for you, no worries. Try a different one. But you will never know what will work if you do not get started.

Knowing which social media to choose is going to depend largely on your intentions for using it, your target audience, your personality and your content. There are a lot of articles and discussions online surrounding this topic. Do some exploring, choose ONE, then begin.

Since this book concentrates on the steps in getting set up in order to get you going, we are going to just dip our toe into the waters of social media. We will mainly focus on physically setting up social media accounts. Gaining a social media following is an entirely different topic, and since I am just in the beginning stages of growing my social media networks this will not be a topic that I will be covering.

I am going to give you a brief overview of some of the most widely used social media sites, then provide you with direction on how to get setup on each. The most likely way you will learn about the social media avenue that you choose is to get started.

Engaging in social media can be like standing in quicksand; it is very easy to get sucked in and have no time left for your craft. In order to effectively use social media you must be consistent, but set limits in order to protect yourself from wasting valuable time.

a) Some Social Media Channels
Here is a brief summary of some popular social media channels.

Facebook
Over a billion people use *Facebook*. This is a great social media avenue for engaging in conversation, posting videos & pictures and sharing other content and links.

Twitter
Twitter is excellent for delivering short news type information and sharing quick messages. *Twitter* is what is called a live feed, which means the messages appear in your stream as they are posted. "Tweets," as they are called in the *Twitter* world, are messages that are 140 characters or less and are used to interact in this social network. Links to online articles and other information can be included in the tweets. *Twitter* also supports image and video sharing.

LinkedIn

LinkedIn is similar to *Facebook* but with a focus on connecting professionals and businesses.

Pinterest

This social media avenue is mainly used for displaying (called pinning) photos and videos, and looking at other people's ideas and interests. *Pinterest* users are predominantly female.

Setting up on Social Media

IMPORTANT: Be sure to read through and understand all terms of service before signing up for any social media.

Note: Always logout of your social media accounts at the end of your sessions.

b) How to Create a Facebook Author or Business Page

Facebook persists in being one of the most popular choices for social media, so that is where we are going to start. Assuming you already have a *Facebook* account, the setup of an author or small business page is very simple and will have you up and running in moments.

The following steps will walk you through setting up a Facebook author or small business page:

STEP 1

Log into your *Facebook* account. If you do not have an account, go to www.facebook.com and fill in the information on that page in order to set one up.

STEP 2

Click on the little dropdown arrow which is in the far right of the top menu bar.

STEP 3

Click on "create page."

STEP 4

Choose from the available page types.

STEP 5

Choose a category from the list in the dropdown menu. Enter your name or business name. Read through the terms and agreements.

STEP 6

Click "Get Started."

You will now find your authors page (or whatever page you just set up) listed on the side of your home page. Click on it to view. You can now post updates and interact with your readers, followers or customers.

You can change your profile picture, banner picture, and write a description of your endeavor in the about section, all under your *Facebook* "settings."

Watch the following video to see how to set up a *Facebook* author's page:

https://youtu.be/dUZzyN3I-gc

c) How to Get Set Up on Twitter

Getting set up on Twitter is very simple, it just takes a few quick steps:

STEP 1

Go to http://www.twitter.com

In the *Sign up* box enter the requested information then click "Sign up for Twitter."

STEP 2

On the next page, you will be prompted through options such as choosing a stronger password and staying signed in on your computer.

STEP 3

Click "create my account."

Your account is now created.

You will now be led through the steps of choosing people to follow.

STEP 4

Twitter will send you an email verification so be sure to verify your account.

STEP 5

Click on the empty profile photo in order to upload your picture.

Click on the area below your profile picture and write a short biography.

To make additional edits to your profile, click the "Edit Profile" button on the top right of your profile on your home page.

STEP 6

Begin to tweet! Tweets are *Twitter* messages: they have a maximum of 140 characters. Tweets can be used in many ways such as giving advice, sending out inspirations or encouragements, marketing products, joining in conversations and connecting with others.

In the *Twitter* world, you are identified by what is called a *Twitter handle*. It is the username preceded immediately by the @ symbol. For instance, my *Twitter* handle is @MelanieAFischer . I invite you to connect with me on *Twitter*. A *Twitter* message would look something like this: "@MelanieAFischer I just wanted to say hello. I am working through your book and now I am learning how to use Twitter." Just remember that your messages need to be no more than 140 characters, including the *Twitter handle*.

See you on *Twitter*!

Now that you are set up on *Twitter*, some great resources to teach you the basics is Ruth Snyder's Kindle books: *Learn Twitter: 10 Beginning Steps (Authors' Social Media Mastery Series)* and *Learn Twitter: 10 Intermediate Steps (Authors' Social Media Mastery Series Book 2)*
http://www.amazon.com/gp/product/B00VFETELG

http://www.amazon.com/Learn-Twitter-Intermediate-Authors-Mastery-ebook/dp/B00ZBRTYTU/

d) Get Set Up with LinkedIn

LinkedIn takes a bit more effort and strategy to get set up. It works well to have your updated resume beside you when setting up *LinkedIn* in order to know what information to put into your profile.

To get set up on LinkedIn:
STEP 1
Go to http://www.linkedin.com
STEP 2
Fill in all of the required information on this *Get Started* page.
STEP 3
Change your privacy settings by turning off your activity broadcasts. By doing this you will not be broadcasting every time you make a change to your profile, which will be very often in this beginning stage and would therefore be annoying to your followers.

You will find this option by hovering over your profile image in the far right of the top menu bar then clicking on "Privacy & Settings."

Under the list of "Privacy Controls" you should see the option: "Turn on/off your activity broadcasts." Unclick the box then save your settings.
STEP 4

Add your information.

Fill in all of the information as you desire. You can add a resume, PDF's, online articles, images and more.
STEP 5

Turn your activity broadcasts back on in your privacy settings when you have completed setting up your profile in order to notify your followers when you make updates to your *LinkedIn* profile.

e) Setting Up on Pinterest

You can set up either a business or personal account with *Pinterest*. If you wish to use your *Pinterest* account for commercial purposes then it is stated in *Pinterest's* terms of service that you **must** create a business account.

Using a *Pinterest* business account allows you to use your business name. This is a good thing because it will increase the visibility of your business.

Getting started on *Pinterest* is fairly straight forward. To set up a personal account, go to http://www.pinterest.com enter the requested information, then follow the setup steps.

To set up a *Pinterest* business account there are two ways to go about it. You can either convert your existing personal account to a business account or start a new one.

To convert your existing Pinterest personal account to a business account:
STEP 1

Log into your existing *Pinterest* account.
STEP 2

Go to the *Pinterest for Business* section.

There you will find a large red button that says "Convert your existing account." Click this button.

STEP 3

You will now be on a page where you will be prompted to "update your public profile information for your business account." Fill in all of the requested information.

In this section you will have to agree to the terms of service agreement and privacy policy. Be sure to read through the terms of service in order to understand what you are agreeing to when you sign up.

If you don't want to convert your existing personal *Pinterest* account to a business account, or you do not have an account yet and want to set up a business account follow these steps.

To set up a Pinterest business account:

STEP 1

Go to https://www.pinterest.com/business/create/

STEP 2

Fill in all of the required information then click "Create account."

STEP 3

Pinterest will then walk you through the steps of choosing boards to follow, setting up your profile, and creating your own boards. Be sure to read through the terms of service in order to understand what you are agreeing to when you sign up.

f) Activating the Social Media Buttons on Your Website

Social media buttons are the little images of the logos of social media sites found on websites, which are linked to a person's corresponding social media pages. When these buttons are clicked, you will be taken to wherever it is that the button is linked to. Having links to your social media sites from your website is an excellent way to keep your online community connected and grow your followers, your reach, and your influence.

Many of the *WordPress* themes have social media buttons incorporated in them. What you need to do in that case is insert your social media URL in the appropriate place within your dashboard in order to link the button on your website to your social media site.

The following steps will show you how to activate your social media buttons, assuming you are using a theme for your website that has social media buttons incorporated in it. If not, you will need to install your own social media buttons, which you will learn in section g).

To activate your social media buttons on your website:
STEP 1

Log into your *WordPress* Dashboard.
STEP 2

Hover over "Appearance" in your side menu bar.
STEP 3

In the pop out menu, you may find a *settings* option for your theme. This will likely be labelled as the name of your theme then the word *settings*. For instance, if the theme which you are using is "Parabola" then you would find "Parabola Settings" in the Appearance pop out menu.

Note: Themes will vary so you may need to snoop around your *WordPress* dashboard in order to find your social media options/settings. The following video will give some ideas of where you may find this.

STEP 4

If your theme incorporates social media buttons then you will likely find an option for social media settings on this theme-settings page. Click on *social media settings.*

Note: If your theme does not include social media buttons, the next section will show you how to place social media buttons onto your website.

STEP 5

In the social media settings section, find the spot where you are to enter the URL for each of your social media sites. Then copy your social media public URL and paste it into the appropriate spot which corresponds to that particular social media.

Use your *public URL* for your social media sites. Be sure NOT to publish the URL of your admin page. The help section in each social media site should have information on how to find your public URL.
STEP 6

Make your preferred selections for your social media options. These options may include, where on your website you would like your social media buttons placed. You may also have the option as to whether or not you would like your social media site to open in a new window. It is a good idea to have it open in a new window in order to minimize the chances of your viewer navigating away from your website.

Watch the following video to see how to activate the social media buttons on your website:

https://youtu.be/fLsVZE0kkEY

g) Installing Social Media Buttons

If your theme does not include social media buttons you will need to install them yourself. This may sound daunting, but it isn't too bad and it is very beneficial to have these buttons on your website.

Watch the following video to see how to install social media buttons onto your website if you do not have these buttons in your theme:

https://youtu.be/ew8Bcv8cbH4

h) Some Notes on Social Media

Social media sites can change their policies and pull the plug on your business campaigns if your business tactics do not line up with their terms and conditions. It is recommended to NOT put all of your eggs in one basket. It is a good idea to always direct your traffic to your website, and optimally to your opt-in box, so that even if your social media avenue comes to a halt, you would not lose all of your followers.

i) Social Networking for Writers and Readers

There are additional online networking channels that are often used that are not necessarily thought of as *social media*, yet they support a culture of sharing and online socializing. Such an avenue that is geared towards readers and writers is *Goodreads*.

Goodreads is an Amazon company. It is a free site where readers and authors can share their book experiences with one another. Readers can search for titles they are interested in reading, read and give reviews, interact with authors and more. Authors can create a profile to promote their written works and interact with their readers.

Sign up on the *Goodreads* website to get started.

If you have a book published, the *Goodreads* author program is well worth joining. To sign up for the *Goodreads* author program, find the "author program" button on the *Goodreads* website, click and get started.

Another opportunity for readers and authors to connect is through online book retailers. To get started, go to Amazon.com or any other online book retailer and sign up for an account. These sites generally have an enormous community of readers. Where there are readers, of course there are authors also. If you have any books published it is a good idea to sign up for an author's page. Do an online search, or search within the specific site, for instructions on how to set up an author page with your chosen online book retailer.

CHAPTER 9

Plank 5: Video

Video opens up a whole new set of doors. This may seem like an entryway that only the "techy" whizzes can go through, but that is not at all the case. There are many apps and software that take the mystery out of video. Many of these options are quite straight forward to use and are reasonably priced. Of course you can go all the way, as with anything, and invest umpteen dollars and a bazillion hours. But we are going to learn just enough here to get you over the threshold and into the arms of Mr. Video (or Mrs. Video).

a) Setting Up on YouTube

In order to display the videos that you create, you will need to choose a video platform that you can upload them to. The most popular video platform is *YouTube*. *YouTube* is owned by *Google* and has A LOT of visitors, so it is a very good place to start. You can certainly explore other options but we are going to stick to *YouTube* in this classroom since most people start here.

To get set up on YouTube:

STEP 1

In order to upload videos to *YouTube* you will need to have a *YouTube* account. Since *Google* owns *YouTube*, if you have a *Google* account you already have a *YouTube* account. If you have a *Gmail* account, *Blogger* account, or are set up on any of *Googles* other services you have a *Google* account. Your login information will be the same for all of these accounts unless you have made changes to them. Go to http://www.youtube.com and click on "Sign in" at the top right hand corner. You will then be prompted to sign in with your *Google* account information. If you do not have a *Google* account you will need to set one up.

STEP 2

When you log into *YouTube* for the first time you will have an opportunity to select channels to subscribe to.

What is a *YouTube* channel you ask?

A *YouTube* channel is the home page for a *YouTube* account that someone has set up. This is where the account name and type will appear, as well as all of the public videos that have been uploaded by the person that created this *YouTube* account.

Without a channel you will only be able to subscribe to channels and "like" and "dislike" videos. You guessed it; if you want to upload videos, you will need to set up a channel. This is done by clicking on "channel" which you will probably find in the top right corner, then follow the prompts to set it up.

STEP 3

You can customize the look of your channel to match your theme or brand by uploading a picture, banner, and/or logo. To do so, click on the little pencil in the banner area that appears when you move your mouse on top of it.

You can modify your *YouTube* channel as you develop your brand. For now, get set up the best you can, then prepare to learn as you go.

b) Making Videos and Uploading Them to YouTube

Now you are ready to upload videos. But of course you need videos to upload. There are many ways to make them. An easy type to make is called a "talking head" video, which is literally a video of a headshot talking (typically yourself). Using this type of video, you can make an intro to your website or "explainer" videos. One way to do this is to go to your *YouTube* channel, click on the "upload" button which you will likely find in the top right hand corner, then click "webcam capture" in the create videos section—this will work assuming you have a webcam and microphone built into your computer, or you have an external webcam and speakers set up.

Another way to make a "talking head" video and upload it to your *YouTube* channel is with your mobile device. Just whip out your smartphone or tablet (assuming you have one) and record a video of yourself talking. Once your video is complete, there should be an export icon to click on (likely a little box with an arrow coming out of it). The option for *YouTube* should appear on the list of choices. Sign into your *YouTube* account when prompted to do so on your device. Follow the prompts and complete the video upload to your *YouTube* channel. That is it!

If you have a video saved on your computer, you can upload it to *YouTube* also. To do this, from your channel, click the "Upload" button. Click on "Select files to upload" then choose the desired file from your computer.

There are many video making apps and software available. I will go into this a bit in the *Creating a Book Trailer* section below.

IMPORTANT: If you are uploading a video that is not ALL your own content, you will need to have permission for all of the content that is in the video. This would include of course the video itself,

but also the music and text or spoken words that are used. Be sure to read through the Terms of Use before uploading any videos and understand the legal limitations when it comes to video sharing. You must be very aware of Copyright when sharing videos. Get familiar with what you can and cannot do when it comes to sharing videos online.

To learn more about video creation, check out the tutorial videos at the end of this chapter on creating videos.

c) A Little More YouTube Video Info

When uploading a video on *YouTube*, you have an option of sharing it publically, privately or unlisted. You will be prompted to choose one of these settings when you upload your video.

Public

Public means that anyone can see it.

Private

Private means that the video will not appear on your channel or in search results. The viewer will need a password in order to view a private video. There is a limit as to how many people may see a private video.

Unlisted

An unlisted video will not appear in any of *YouTube's* public search results or on your channel. Only people who have the URL can access the video, so you will need to provide the link to those whom you want to view the video. There is no limit on how many people can watch an unlisted video. There is no guarantee that someone whom you have not provided the link wouldn't stumble upon an unlisted video.

There are limitations on the size and length of a video that can be up-loaded to *YouTube*. *YouTube* videos generally cannot be more than 15 minutes long. There are ways around that, but for the most part short videos are the most engaging. It is best to stick with making 1-3 minute videos. If you do find it necessary to make longer videos, understand the limitations before creating them.

d) Creating a Book Trailer

An exciting video option for authors is a *book trailer*. A **book trailer** is similar to a movie trailer; it exhibits a particular book and is used for pro-motional purposes. A way that I have found to be fairly simple in making a book trailer is with my iPad. Of course there are other tablets out there as well. There are thousands and thousands of apps available that you can use with various tablets—the ideas are endless. An **app** is a program or a piece of software that has been designed for a specific purpose (such as for creating videos), which are available for download to your mobile device through the *App Store*. Some are free and some have a cost. Explore on-line for options and search through the apps in the App Store. If you are using an *Apple* device you will need to set up an *iTunes* account in order to download apps. There are also oodles of movie/video making software and online programs available that do not require a tablet.

We couldn't possibly look at all of the video options, that would take a lifetime. There are many forums and blogs on video creation. Do some online searches and get creative.

A good video-making app to start with, if you happen to be using an *Apple* device, is *iMovie*—it is a fairly straight forward movie maker. There are video trailer templates available in *iMovie* that allow you to take video footage and drop it into various spots within the template to create an effective trailer.

The app that was used to make the *Ya…But How?* book trailer is called *VideoScribe*—a whiteboard animation tool. If you have not yet seen the trailer for this book, or would like a refresher, take a look at it here:

http://youtu.be/xd28UdTtVAs

VideoScribe is available as an app for mobile devices, as well as available online. I will show you how to create a book trailer using the online version of *VideoScribe,* in the tutorial video at the end of this chapter.

e) Putting Your Videos onto Your Website

Once you have created your video(s) and uploaded them to *YouTube,* follow these steps to put them onto your website:

STEP 1

Log into your *YouTube* account.

STEP 2

Click "My Channel" from the side menu.

STEP 3

Click "videos" from the menu bar that is under your banner.

STEP 4

Click on your desired video.

STEP 5

Click the "video manager" button which is in the menu bar directly below your video.

STEP 6

Click the "edit" button beside your desired video.

STEP 7

To the right of your video you should see a text box that has the video URL in it. Click the video URL to highlight it then right click and copy.

STEP 8

Log into the Dashboard of your website then go to the page or post where you would like to insert your video. There will be tabs for either visual or text for your entry. When you are inserting code, such as for videos, remember to insert it into the text tab, (I know that this may sound counterintuitive because a video is a visual but trust me, it goes under the text tab since URL's are a form of code). Put the curser where you would like to insert your video. Right click and paste. The code for the video should now appear.

STEP 9

Click the "Update" button on the page. If you do not update the page it will not save this change.

STEP 10

Visit your website as it would be viewed by the general public (the front-end) to ensure that your video shows up in the desired spot.

This is probably one of the most exciting accomplishments for a "techy" newbie...so it is ok if you do a happy dance! You can even capture it on video if you like and upload it to *YouTube*.

Feel free to get some video creating ideas from the videos which I've created. You can check out my *YouTube* channel at: https://www.youtube.com/channel/UC5Gv3cRwW3iDrJmsKrg1COg

Watch the following tutorial video on how to create your video in *VideoScribe*:

https://youtu.be/D-dL_22VtWM

To sign up online for *VideoScribe*—a whiteboard video animation tool—go to: http://www.videoscribe.co You can choose to begin with a free trial or go straight to a subscription! You will also find *VideoScribe* in an app store for your mobile device.

Here is the sample video that we just created in the tutorial video using *VideoScribe*: https://youtu.be/s44z7yc-3v8

Watch the following video to see how to upload your videos to *YouTube*:

https://youtu.be/qgjxavjGR1o

Now that you have a rough idea of how to build your own videos and trailers, you can explore online for video making tools or pull out your iPad (or another suitable technology) and start playing around with ideas. Rather than spending a Friday night watching reruns, you now have something else you can do!

SECTION THREE:

Wrapping It Up

CHAPTER 10

Wrap It Up

Congratulations! You have navigated your way across the canyon of "Ya…But How?" Take a look back and see how far you have come. Celebrate your success and reflect on what you have learned from the probable blunders you encountered along the way.

As you can see, much can be achieved by pushing forward and not giving up. It takes persistence, perseverance and courage to live life the way you were created to. We don't live on *purpose* by *accident*.

https://youtu.be/pS4vpvrr_6c

a) Would You Give a Book Review?

I'll even provide you with instructions on how to do so!

Why are book reviews so important?

An author pours sweat and tears into their book creations. And then, they take the leash off their hard work and release it into the busy marketplace. Sometimes we hear from our readers, but often not. In order to get back to our desks and onto another creation that will serve our readers, it sure is helpful to hear how we did.

And...sometimes, online advertising streams and book review sites requires there to be a certain number of positive reviews on retailer sites before they will consider allowing the author ad space.

If you found this book *Ya...But How?* helpful, I would truly appreciate if you provided a review. If you have a word for improvement, I welcome that as well. In the end, book reviews serve the reader also. They encourage your favorite authors to continue writing, and feedback improves future books for your reading enjoyment.

How to write a Book Review:

STEP 1

Go to Amazon.com or any other online book retailer. Sign in. If you have not yet signed up for an account, you can do so now.

STEP 2

Enter the title of the book which you would like to give the review for into the search box.

STEP 3

You should now be on a page with a list of books with that title. Click on the book that you are looking for.

STEP 4

Directly under the book title and author name you will see 5 stars and a link such as "25 customer reviews." Click on that link to bring you to the reviews.

STEP 5

Scroll down until you find the "Write a customer review" button. Click.

STEP 6

Write your review.

It is a good idea to write it in a word processer, such as *Word*, then copy and paste into this space. This would save you from extreme frustration in the unfortunate case of losing your review before it gets published.

How to write a Book Review in Goodreads:

STEP 1

Go to goodreads.com and sign in. If you have not yet signed up for a Goodreads account you can do so now.

STEP 2

Search for the book title that you would like to write a book review on—type the desired book title into the search box.

STEP 3

You should now be on a page with a list of books with that title (or closely related titles). To the right of the book, you can rate it. Once you give it a rating, the status label above the stars will change to "read"— hover over this and an option will appear to "write a review." Click on "Write a review."

STEP 4

Write your review and share it.

Note: A good review is kept fairly short—about 200 words or less. It is honest and is written in a positive manner, even if the review isn't entirely positive.

b) Ya...But Now What?

Great question!

Your platform is built—now it is time to switch your focus to learn how to use it in order to grow your audience.

The best resource that I know of to teach you the next phase of platform building is the book ***Platform: Get noticed in a noisy world by Michael Hyatt.*** Check out Michael Hyatt's book here: http://michaelhyatt.com/platform

Wherever your online ventures bring you, staying fuelled up on *purpose* is what will keep you going. Living with purpose is being mindful of your gifts and abilities, and serving the world with them. It is easy to get side tracked though and forget to live purposefully. Let's face it, we live in a noisy and distracting world. That is why I send out *crumbs of purpose,* mini inspirations every few days to remind you to stay committed to living a life filled with meaning and intention.

If you are hungry for purpose, get your crumbs of purpose at my home page http://www.hungryforpurpose.com. Sign up now and you will also receive my short video "3 solutions for purposeful living."

And then...

...dish up my weekly blog—short lessons that use simple analogies to teach about living with purpose: http://www.hungryforpurpose.com/blog

As you move forward in this journey, continue to think and pray your way through. Keep marching onward! Even when diversions fall onto your path, endure in finding ways for your online platform to be a part of your life purpose!

Many blessings on all your life ventures!

I strive to serve content that will satisfy your hunger to live a life of purpose!

To be notified when new material comes out, fill out one of those handy dandy opt-in boxes at: http://www.hungryforpurpose.com/whats-new/

To pump some enthusiasm and inspiration into your next conference... invite me to present a workshop, short talk or keynote presentation!

Head on over to the events and services page for details on my topics of presentations: http://www.hungryforpurpose.com/eventsservices/

Does the thought of writing your own material for your website freak you out?

Understandably so. A website is only as good as the message that is on it. No worries! As a trained copywriter, I can write website copy and other material for you. Specializing in content creation, I develop material like this instructional book. Such content gives your business leverage in propelling your purpose filled works into the hearts of your targeted audience.

Have me create for you:

- Website copy
- Instructional books like this one
- Promotional video scripts
- Blog posts
- And more...

Check out my copywriting services at: http://www.WritingForPurpose.com and click on "Get Great Copy Now" to get started!

Resources

The links to the following services are *affiliate* links. This means that if you purchase the service through an affiliate link, you will gift me with a commission on your purchase. I would greatly appreciate your support! There will be no interference to the service that you will receive if you choose to use these links. Be assured, I am only an affiliate to services which I have used and have been greatly satisfied with.

Web host provider
Blue Host: http://www.bluehost.com/track/hungryforpurpose

Email marketing service
AWeber: http://aweber.com/?425455

Other Resources

For the most up-to-date list of resources check out my resources page at: http://www.hungryforpurpose.com/resources/

For my latest books and other items to equip you to live your life on purpose visit: http://www.hungryforpurpose.com/books

Great resources to teach you Twitter basics are Ruth Snyder's Kindle books: *Learn Twitter: 10 Beginning Steps (Authors' Social Media Mastery Series)* and *Learn Twitter: 10 Intermediate Steps (Authors' Social Media Mastery Series Book 2)*
    http://www.amazon.com/gp/product/B00VFETELG

http://www.amazon.com/Learn-Twitter-Intermediate-Authors-Mastery-ebook/dp/B00ZBRTYTU/

GLOSSARY

Note: Some of these definitions may have different meanings in everyday language, and therefore may not be the official definitions of these words. These are definitions that are most suitable for the context of this book.

Admin URL: The URL that you will need to type into the web browser in order to access the administration end of your website in order to make changes to your website and post new content. Your admin URL will look something like this: www.(yourname).com/wp-admin

App: A program or a piece of software that has been designed for a specific purpose (such as for creating movies), which are available for download to your mobile device through an *App Store*.

Autoresponder: A system or program, such as an email marketing service, which delivers a series of email messages automatically.

Back-end: The administration end of an online service. This is where you will be making all of your changes—an area which is not accessible to the general public (Often called the dashboard).

Blog: Typically a web page which frequently has new content added to it (in forms of posts)—like a journal.

Blog broadcast: A means in which a blog is sent out to an email list automatically each time a new blog post is made—this is done using an email marketing provider.

Blog page: A web page which has the capability of having new information added to it (called *posts*)—the old information remains available in a library or archives like a list of journal entries, typically displayed in order, starting from the most recent (may also be called a *posting page*).

Blog post: An entry that is put into a blog then remains available in archives which can be accessed even when new posts are added (may be referred to simply as a "post").

Book trailer: A short video, similar to a movie trailer, which exhibits a particular book and is used for promotional purposes.

Broadcast: A message, which is created within an email marketing service (such as *AWeber*), that is sent out to a particular list—the message can be sent out immediately or may be scheduled to go out at a later date and time.

CMS (Content Management System): A CMS is a web application that makes it easy to add, edit and manage a website.

Dashboard: What many services, such as *WordPress,* calls the screen where you can make changes and add content; the dashboard is usually the first screen you will see when logging into a particular online service (often referred to as the back-end).

Domain name: The registered website name. Also referred to as the *web address.*

Domain suffix: The last portion of a domain name. Popular examples of these are .com, .org, .net

Email list: A list of emails which have been electronically collected and compiled, with permission, when people subscribe for particular information—this email list can then be used for email marketing.

Email marketing: When messages offering products, services or other forms of communication are sent to a group of people (a list) by use of email.

Email marketing service (or email marketing provider): An online service that is used to collect and manage emails.

Follow up series: A sequence of messages which are sent out to a particular list through your email marketing service—may also be referred to as an email campaign.

Front-end: Generally refers to the web pages which are viewable by the general public, as opposed to the back-end of the website where you will be making your changes.

Hosted website: A website that will be hosted on a server for you.

Mobile responsive: A website that has been designed for optimal viewing, navigating and interacting on mobile devices.

Online Platform: An umbrella term used to describe the combination of all the *online devices* which are being used to help make your works known. A platform typically has two parts 1) The *physical components,* such as: a blog, podcast and social media channels 2) The *people* whom you have influence on, such as: members of online groups you are part of, your social media followers, blog subscribers and podcast listeners. Your platform ultimately is the *people* you have influence on, but without the physical means of reaching out, it would be difficult to connect with them.

Opt-in Box: A box on a web page where information such as a name and email is entered in exchange for something, such as a newsletter or an ebook. This may also be called a *sign up form.*

Platform: An umbrella term used to describe the combination of ALL (online and offline) devices which are being used to help make your works known. A platform typically has two parts 1) The *physical components,* such as: a blog, podcast, social media channels, live workshops 2) The *people* whom you have influence on, such as: members of a group or a club you are part of, your social media followers, blog subscribers and podcast listeners. Your platform ultimately is the *people* you have influence on, but without the physical means of reaching out, it would be difficult to connect with them.

Plugin: An additional piece of software that can be installed on a website in order to add features and modifications.

Self-hosted website: A website that hosting on a server is NOT provided for you.

Server: Generally a third party tower of computer-like hardware that stores electronic files. Typically used to store websites and all of its content.

Social media: Online channels that are used to socially interact within virtual communities—may also be referred to as *Social Networks.*

Static page: A web page that has information that does not change except for necessary updates—examples of these would be a *contact* page and an *about* page.

Theme: A theme for a website is basically a template—it is what gives your website a specific look and feel to the presentation of your content. The theme lays out the *basic* website design and function.

URL: Uniform Resource Locator—this is your web address: the terms URL, website, web address and domain all tend to be used interchangeably.

Web host provider: A service which provides a place (a server) for your website to be stored.

Web hosting: Having your website stored (hosted) on a server in order for it to be accessed over the internet.

Web pages: Individual pages within a website, such as: an about page, a blog page, a contact page and so on.

Acknowledgments

To my husband Lance whom without this project would have remained an "idea."

To my mom who gave me life and inspires me to live it.

To my daughter Ashley who I have grown with and have learned more from than seems possible for a mother to learn from her child.

To the other children in my life, Cody, Hunter and Shawna, who have given me many reasons to keep going.

To my sister Lynell who has made it crystal clear that I am to never give up on my purpose.

To my brother Kevin, whose simple words "just do it," are often all I need to hear.

To my mentor and coach Sheila Webster who helped me get my feet unstuck from the cement of fear and uncertainty.

To all my friends and family who have, and continue to, smother me in love and prayer throughout my seemingly endless writing endeavours.

To all those who will forgive me for not mentioning you by name, who have influenced, encouraged and motivated me to keep plugging away.

And to our good Lord for creating each and every one of us for a purpose and for giving us the desire to understand and fulfill what that purpose is...and for giving us your son, Jesus Christ, to walk with every step of the way.

And Thank You…
…for giving me the opportunity to teach you how to build your
online platform and move one step closer to living out your purpose!

If you are Hungry for Purpose…come eat!

Melanie Fischer
MelanieFischer@HungryForPurpose.com
http://www.hungryforpurpose.com
@MelanieAFischer

NOTES

NOTES

www.ingramcontent.com/pod-product-compliance
Lightning Source LLC
Chambersburg PA
CBHW071219050326
40689CB00011B/2373